Lavender, Rosemary,

Peppermint,

and Sage

Lavender, Parsley, Peppermint, and Sage

Herbal Solutions for Every Household

All-Natural, Earth-Friendly Projects and Problem-Solvers for Health and Home

Shea Zukowski

METRO BOOKS
New York

METRO BOOKS
New York

An Imprint of Sterling Publishing
387 Park Avenue South
New York, NY 10016

Illustrations © 2011 by **p9, 54, 57, 63, 119:** © iStockphoto.com/Song Speckels; **p20, 42, 128, 133, 135, 144, 145, 147, 149, 151, 153, 154, 156, 163, 164, 179, 198:** © iStockphoto.com/Kathy Konkle; **p23:** © iStockphoto.com/Kateryna Davydenko; **p24, 71, 108:** © iStockphoto.com/bubaone; **p28, 30, 34, 44, 58, 65, 72, 88, 92, 106, 109, 125, 126, 139, 142, 155, 158, 168, 180, 182, 191, 194:** © iStockphoto.com/Thomas Young; **p36, 60:** © iStockphoto.com/Olga Axyutina; **p46:** © iStockphoto.com/bortonia; **p49, 98, 115, 160, 192:** © iStockphoto.com/Helga Jaunegg; **p62, 75, 112:** © powerHousePackaging/Lynne Yeamans; **p68:** © iStockphoto.com/wmiran; **p80, 177:** © iStockphoto.com/Vera Kalinovska; **p82, 150, 187:** © iStockphoto.com/Heidi Kalyani; **p87, 90, 93, 105:** © iStockphoto.com/Claudelle Girard; **p110, 131:** © iStockphoto.com/Татьяна Прибытько; **p137:** © iStockphoto.com/Natural_Warp; **p184, 189:** © iStockphoto.com/Mehmet Ali Cida

This 2011 edition published by Metro Books by arrangement with
powerHouse Packaging & Supply, Inc.

Design by Lynne Yeamans

ISBN 978-1-4351-3722-6 (print format)   ISBN 978-1-4351-3871-1 (ebook)

For information about custom editions, special sales, and premium and corporate purchases, please contact Sterling Special Sales at 800-805-5489 or specialsales@sterlingpublishing.com.

Manufactured in the United States of America

2 4 6 8 10 9 7 5 3 1

www.sterlingpublishing.com

Though we endorse a green lifestyle, the publisher, packager, and author disclaim any liability from any harm, loss, or injury that may result from the use, proper or improper, of the information contained in this book. We advise that common sense dictate any use of the formulas and do not claim that the information contained herein is complete or accurate for your situation. This book is intended as a reference volume only, not as a medical manual. The information given here is designed to help you make informed decisions about your health. It is not intended as a substitute for any treatment that may have been prescribed by your doctor.

Acknowledgments

In researching my previous book, *Salt, Lemons, Vinegar, and Baking Soda*, it was exciting to realize how many other simple ways there are to achieve a cleaner, more natural lifestyle. Just a handful of herbs or a few drops of essential oil, for example, can offer new ways to a cleaner, greener home. I took careful note of the many different options out there, and the best of those ideas have been distilled into the book you now hold in your hands.

Research aside, it would have seemed foolish to expect another book to come together as smoothly as the first, but again I found myself delightfully surprised by the amazing people who helped bring this project to fruition. Specifically, I'd like to thank Denise McGann at Sterling Publishing, Inc., for seeing the opportunities another title would present.

Likewise, the wonderful team at powerHouse Packaging proved once again good things come in small packages, including Sharyn Rosart for her clear editorial vision of the project and enthusiasm at every turn; Lynne Yeamans for providing a fresh and inspiring design (yet again!) that made it a pleasure to turn every page; and editors extraordinaire Erin Canning and Hallie Einhorn, plus Sterling's Stephanie Nikolopoulos, who suggested many valuable ways to make the advice in this book as clear and easy-to-follow as possible.

Lastly, my deepest appreciation goes to my family, Stan, Isaiah, and Eli, who cheer me on with their boundless enthusiasm and bring me coffee when I need it most.

Contents

Part 2: YOUR HERBAL HOME   123

Preface

HAVE YOU EVER FOUND THAT A CUP OF CHAMOMILE TEA BEFORE BED HELPS YOU TO FALL ASLEEP FASTER? Perhaps the fresh scent of lemons puts a little pep in your step? Or maybe you smelled the unmistakable odor of clove–while in your dentist's office? You are already harnessing the amazing power of herbs in your daily life. And you are not alone. For thousands of years, countless people have turned to herbs as a means to better, more healthful living.

Today, as people have become more earth-conscious, there are more easy ways than ever to enjoy the power of the plant world and to make better use of many herbal items you may already have around the house. This book aims to serve as your guide in expanding your herbal pursuits. The first half of this book shows you how to utilize the power of common herbs that can help you feel and look better. You will find dozens of simple, easy-to-prepare remedies for everything from upset stomach to dry skin to insomnia.

However, the power of herbs extends far beyond your medicine chest! The same antibacterial and antiviral properties that make herbs so valuable to human health can have great benefit in keeping your home clean and fresh. In the second half of this book, you will find a wealth of useful ways to tap into many of those same herbs to improve the state of things around the house.

If you have never used herbs before, this book is an excellent place to start. Before you try any of the ideas that follow, however, make sure you read the introductory sections on Using Herbs Wisely (page 16) and How to Make Your Own Teas and Tinctures (page 18). Do consult the safe-use guidelines on page 202. While side effects are rare, a few of the herbs may be inadvisable for some people.

If you have some common herbs in your pantry, or a few lavender plants ready to bloom in your garden, you may be ready to begin— if not, you'll find most of the herbs and herbal products mentioned in this book at your local grocer or health-products store. Choose a couple of formulas you'd like to try and get started!

—SHEA ZUKOWSKI

INTRODUCTION

The Amazing Power of Herbs

A Brief History of Herbal Medicine

AS JUST ABOUT ANY HERBAL EXPERT WILL TELL YOU, our relationship with herbs is as long as the history of mankind itself, growing out of our need to survive in the natural world. Anthropologists suspect that our earliest ancestors were adept at paying close attention to the plants and animals around them to figure out (largely through trial and error) such useful knowledge as which herbs could help preserve food and which could promote healing. In essence, herbal wisdom developed out of our collective quest for life itself and is tied to our earliest understanding of the study of medicine.

In 1874, Egyptologists discovered what is believed to be the world's oldest medical text just outside Luxor. It is a sixty-five-foot (20-m) scroll (now referred to as the Ebers Papyrus) that is estimated to have been around since 1500 BCE. This amazing document lists 876 herbal formulas derived from more than 500 herbs. Some of the remedies described in that text may seem crazy to us now (does anyone really want to try a shampoo made from a donkey hoof?), but others would be recognizable to herbalists today.

In 1991, a team of hikers in the Italian Alps stumbled across the frozen remains of a prehistoric man who is estimated to have died there some 5,300 years ago. Among his equipment and supplies were a couple of mushrooms that turned out to be a particular species containing a compound that can fight intestinal parasites. Later, when performing an autopsy on the body, scientists were amazed to discover that the Iceman's digestive tract contained the eggs of an intestinal parasite. This evidence would suggest that people were practicing herbal medicine roughly 1,800 years before the Ebers Papyrus was created.

Since using herbs for health and home is clearly nothing new, how did we arrive at what is today a multibillion-dollar industry? To understand the answer to that question, we need to consider how drug companies capitalized on herbal wisdom in the first place with one of the most venerable stories in modern medicine, the development of aspirin.

We know that by around 500 BCE, Chinese physicians relied on the bark of the white willow tree to provide pain relief to their patients. Almost five hundred years later, that information had traveled to Europe, where herbal healers used the plant to treat a wide variety of conditions. It wasn't until the seventeenth century that English herbalists hit upon the idea of pulverizing the bark into a fine powder to brew a bitter tea. They were looking for a cure for malaria when they first brewed willow bark tea; while it didn't cure malaria, the herbalists did find that it had a remarkable ability to reduce fevers in those afflicted with this dreaded disease.

By 1828, modern chemistry had advanced to the point where scientists could identify and extract the bark's active compound, salicin. A few years later, that same compound was found in another herb, meadowsweet. However, while salicin proved effective at fighting fevers, it also brought with it a host of side effects, including nausea, bleeding, and (at high doses) even death.

Clearly further refinements were necessary, so scientists spent years tinkering with the plant-based chemical they had found, eventually adding other molecules to the mix until they arrived at a synthesized

Do You Know...

WHAT THE DIFFERENCE BETWEEN AN HERB AND A SPICE IS?

Technically speaking, plant scientists consider herbs to be the fresh and dried leaves of plants that grow in temperate zones, so they are usually green in color. Spices, on the hand, are derived from the flowers, fruit, seeds, bark, and roots typically of tropical plants; they range from brown to black to red in color. Some plants are valued for both their leaves and their roots, so one of these may be considered both an herb and a spice, depending on the part being used. In lay terms, however, natural medicine experts generally use "herb" to refer to all plants that have beneficial properties, and so that is the term used throughout this book.

drug they named acetylsalicylic acid. Knowing the general public would require a name that was easier to pronounce, the scientists decided to borrow the "a" from the word "acetyl" and add it to "spirin" (from meadowsweet's genus name, *Spiraea*). It would take another fifty years or so before the German drug manufacturer Bayer rolled out its aspirin product to the world. Since then, aspirin has become the household drug of choice for a broad range of everyday complaints.

Understanding the evolution of this particular drug reveals a lot about the difference between herbal medicine and modern science. Whereas the pharmaceutical industry seeks to isolate select ingredients from our natural world and manipulate them into a powerful and profitable form, the herbal world, for the most part, works with ingredients in as natural a form as possible. As such, herbal products tend to be mild, generally more accessible, and, for the most part, nontoxic. And because herbs often contain several important compounds working together, they are more versatile and able to relieve a number of conditions.

While most herbal experts find value in knowing the active constituents in the plants they use, they also acknowledge that there is still a lot to learn about why certain herbs work as they do. Science has simply not caught up with nature, so we still don't understand exactly how certain compounds interact to produce the results herbalists have noted for centuries.

Using Herbs Wisely

WHILE IT IS WONDERFUL TO THINK OF ALL THE WAYS PLANTS CAN PROVIDE A NATURAL PATH TO WELL-BEING, it is important to point out that herbal experts do suggest a few words of general caution to ensure you are using them wisely.

- **DO WORK WITH YOUR DOCTOR** if you are nursing, pregnant, undergoing treatment for an ongoing condition, or taking any prescription medications. While rare, herb-drug interactions are possible, and your doctor is best equipped to help you select the options that are best for you.

- **DO USE CARE WHERE CHILDREN ARE CONCERNED.** While generally safe, the remedies described in this book are intended for adults. Always consult your child's pediatrician before trying any remedy in this book and keep any herbal cleaning products you make out of reach of children and pets.

- **DO TALK WITH YOUR DOCTOR** if herbal remedies aren't providing you with the relief you need. While herbs have proven their worth for centuries, they are generally milder than other treatments and may not be right for every situation.

- **DO NOT ASSUME THAT MORE IS BETTER.** Follow the directions in this book and do not exceed the boundaries of common sense when it comes to using herbs. If a few cups of mint tea have not resolved your upset stomach, it is unlikely that another ten cups will do the trick.

Organic vs. Conventionally Grown Herbs

If you've perused the aisles of any store's herbal ingredients section, you've likely seen some carrying an "organic" label. What does that label really mean?

Herbal products are cultivated by many different kinds of farmers. Some of them use pesticides and herbicides to protect plants from diseases and pests during the growing season. Others choose to use natural or nonchemical methods of protecting their crops. Unfortunately, many common pesticides and herbicides contain toxic chemicals that often remain on and in the plants they were designed to protect, and those chemicals are then passed along to you, the consumer. It is hard to tell what chemicals may have been used on a particular product unless you see a "certified organic" label, which tells you that it has been grown without synthetic pesticides, herbicides, or fertilizers.

How to Make Your Own Teas and Tinctures

HERBAL TEAS ARE IDEAL FOR DRAWING OUT THE BENEFICIAL PROPERTIES OF AN HERB, and they are among the easiest types of remedies to prepare. There are basically two types of tea-making methods: **infusion** and **decoction**. The choice of method typically depends on which part of the plant is being used.

An infusion is what most people typically associate with tea; it is made from the softer parts of the plant that grow above ground (think leaves and petals). You generally use between 1 to 3 teaspoons (5 to 15 ml) dried herb per 1 cup (240 ml) water.

HOW TO MAKE AN INFUSION

1 to 3 teaspoons (5 to 15 ml) dried herb
1 cup (240 ml) boiling water

Spoon the herb into a cup or pot. Cover with the required amount of boiling water. Allow mixture to steep for 10 to 20 minutes. Pour the steeped brew through a mesh strainer.

A decoction, on the other hand, is used to extract the beneficial compounds from tougher plant material (think bark, berries, and dried roots). The proportion of herb to water is usually a bit more diluted—typically 1 tablespoon (15 ml) herb for 2 cups (475 ml) water. The herbs are allowed to simmer for a longer time, usually 15 to 30 minutes, depending on the remedy.

HOW TO MAKE A DECOCTION

1 tablespoon (15 ml) herb
2 cups (475 ml) water

Place the herbs and water in a covered pot. With the heat on low, allow them to heat up to a gentle bubble. Make sure to keep the lid on the pot to prevent the volatile oils from evaporating as the mixture simmers. Also, keep the pot covered if you allow the mixture to cool to room temperature. Strain before using (or storing, for that matter).

Do You Know...

WHAT THE TERM "VOLATILE" MEANS IN HERBALISM?

In chemistry, "volatile" refers to the tendency of a substance to evaporate at a relatively low temperature. If the essential oils in a particular herb are volatile, they will evaporate during heating. If you keep the lid on the pot while heating, you'll retain those substances in your brew.

Both tea-making methods are excellent to use. Make sure to dispose of any unused quantities after 2 to 3 days.

Tinctures are another effective method for drawing out the healing properties of herbs, and they can extend the shelf life of your healing remedies by a few years.

Tinctures are made by drawing out the beneficial compounds of an herb with alcohol or glycerin. They are more concentrated, so you usually dilute a teaspoon (15 ml) with a glass of water for most remedies. Tinctures are widely available in health-food stores, but if you are inclined to make your own remedies, they are simple enough to prepare with vodka or glycerin. Alcohol is considered more efficient at extracting the properties of herbs, and alcohol-based tinctures have a longer shelf life than glycerin-based mixtures. However, when a nonalcoholic tincture is preferred, glycerin (which can be purchased at health-food stores—be sure to get 100% vegetable glycerin) makes a fine tincture.

HOW TO MAKE A TINCTURE (VODKA)

2 tablespoons (30 ml) herb
5/8 cup, or 5 ounces (150 ml), vodka

Combine 2 tablespoons (30 ml) of your herb and 5/8 cup, or 5 ounces (150 ml), of vodka in a glass jar with a nonmetallic lid. Store in a cool, dark place for 2 to 6 weeks, shaking the jar every day or two to keep contents active. Strain the liquid into another clean jar and store away from light and heat.

HOW TO MAKE A TINCTURE (GLYCERIN)

2 tablespoons (30 ml) herb
1/4 cup, or 2 ounces (60 ml), 100% vegetable glycerin
1/4 cup, or 2 ounces (60 ml), water

Place 2 tablespoons (30 ml) of the herb in a glass jar with a non-metallic lid. Combine the glycerin and water. Pour the glycerin-water mixture into the jar. Close tightly, label, and date. Store the mixture in a cool, dark place for 2 to 6 weeks, shaking the jar every day or two to keep contents active. Strain the liquid into another clean jar and store away from light and heat.

Growing and Drying Your Own Herbs

WHAT IS THE BEST WAY TO ASSURE YOU HAVE ACCESS TO THE FRESHEST HERBS POSSIBLE? Grow your own! Don't have a garden? No problem; you don't need a formal garden space—just a reasonably sunny spot where you can place a couple of containers or a window box.

Calendula, chamomile, lavender, lemon thyme, peppermint, and rosemary are particularly hardy plants easily grown in pots that can be kept indoors or outside (as long as they have access to full sun). Many other herbs can also be grown by the home gardener. Buy your favorite herbs at your local garden store; look for plants that are approximately 3 to 4 inches (7.5 to 10 cm) tall. For best results, plant your herbs in containers that are at least a foot (30.5 cm) wide and have ample drainage holes. Finally, use a potting mix that is formulated for container plants, along with an organic fertilizer.

Once your herbs are thriving, it is time to begin using them. You will want to harvest your herbs when the oils are at their peak. Herbs grown for their leaves should be harvested before they flower. When the plant looks quite leafy, you can feel free to cut up to half of the leaves at one time. If it is herbal flowers you want, cut them just before the plants reach full flower. If you are growing for seeds, harvest as the seedpods turn from green to brown or gray. Be sure to get them before the seedpods open. Herbal roots are best harvested in autumn after the plant's foliage has faded.

After you harvest your herbs, preserve your hard work. Bundle up leafy plants by tying the stems together, then hang them upside down to dry. For seeds, try putting a paper bag around the bottom of the pod, so the seeds are collected as they fall. If you want to pre-serve only the leaves, spread them out on an old window screen to dry. As a general rule, keep your herbs in a warm, dry place with good air circulation and away from the sun (direct sunlight will evaporate their essential oils, rendering them less potent).

Once your herbs are completely dry, store them in airtight containers away from light and heat. Clearly label them and mark the month and date so you know at a glance what is inside each container. And remember, the less the dried herbs are handled, the more they retain their properties.

Aloe vera

Your Guide to Essential Oils

MADE UP OF HUNDREDS OF CHEMICAL COMPOUNDS, an essential oil contains the distinct volatile oils that give the plant it was drawn from its special aroma and flavor. Herbal experts also say essential oils impart antibacterial and antiviral properties, making them valuable resources for both health and home.

To use essential oils wisely, bear in mind that those little bottles of liquid are super-concentrated; it takes sixteen pounds (7 kg) of fresh peppermint to produce an ounce (30 ml) of the plant's essential oil. Because even a drop contains such a concentrated dose, you may experience irritation if an oil is applied directly to your skin. Herbal experts advise diluting essential oils in a carrier oil (e.g., a neutral-

smelling oil like sweet almond oil). In some formulas, however, lavender and tea-tree oils can be safely applied to the skin without dilution. Do avoid getting any essential oil products near your eyes. And while it is true that some essential oils are safely used in commercial foods and health-care items (e.g., mint toothpaste), most essential oils can be highly toxic if swallowed, so do not ingest them. Because they are vulnerable to oxidization, keep essential oils tightly sealed in dark containers away from heat and light.

Herbal Supplements

Herbal supplements (tablets and capsules) have become a very popular alternative to the old-fashioned method of brewing your own teas and tinctures. They may also contain extracts of herbs (the isolated active ingredient), as well as different combinations of herbs in very precise dosages.

That said, the strength and quality among all the supplement products available can vary widely; therefore, the tips and remedies presented in this book rely on using herbs (either fresh or dried) and rendering them into either a tea or tincture. They are also generally cheaper than supplements.

PART 1

Your Herbal Medicine Chest

Herbal Healing

Thyme

LOOKING FOR A MORE NATURAL WAY TO HELP YOUR BODY HEAL ITSELF? You've come to the right place. In the pages that follow, you'll find a variety of home remedies gleaned from reliable sources that can help you tame the pain of a sore throat or toothache, ease the discomfort of a mild burn or upset stomach, and perhaps even speed up your ability to recover from a cold or flu.

If this is your first formal venture into the world of herbal healing, rest assured that what you're about to discover is far from new. Chinese herbalism is considered the oldest herbal tradition because it has the longest unbroken recorded history, and it is still practiced by millions of people worldwide. Likewise, Ayurvedic herbs, drawn from a system based on ancient Hindu traditions, are still widely used in India and other parts of Asia. And long before Europeans made their mark on the New World, Native Americans relied on a wealth of herbal remedies. The classical cultures of ancient Greece and Rome, as well as the ancient Egyptians, used herbs medicinally and documented their use in writing. Down through the ages, the herbal wisdom of our ancestors was shared and used by healers through to modern times. In fact, the World Health Organization estimates that today about 80 percent of the world's population use some form of traditional medicine in their regular self-care, including some very simple herbal remedies like the ones you'll find here.

Dental Remedies

DENTAL DILEMMAS, FROM THE INTENSE PAIN OF A TOOTHACHE TO THE STIGMA OF BAD BREATH are hardly modern-day problems. People have been turning to their herbal medicine chests for hundreds of years to remedy tooth and other mouth-related troubles. Naturally, the purveyors of commercial oral-care products took note, and many of those products contain herbal extracts of mint, cinnamon, clove, and thyme, among others. For treatments you can make at home, your personal herbal dental antidote can be effectively delivered as a gargle, rinse, or compress. All of these are easy to make and require a minimum number of ingredients, which you may already have on hand. That said, as with over-the-counter products, take care not to swallow these remedies unless specifically instructed to do so.

While herbal remedies can help clean your teeth and keep odor-causing germs at bay—some even bolster your regular fluoride treatments— it is important to remember that bad breath and gum disease can signal more serious conditions, such as diabetes and kidney problems, as well as serious decay or gum infection. If you have bleeding, itching gums, tooth pain, or bad breath that isn't relieved after a few days of treatment, schedule an appointment to see your dentist.

OLD-FASHIONED THYME MOUTHWASH

½ cup (120 ml) water

2 tablespoons (30 ml) fresh thyme leaves

1 tablespoon (15 ml) vodka, optional

Thyme possesses strong antiseptic properties and has been used for hundreds of years to treat infections. Bring the water to a gentle boil. Add the thyme leaves and let steep for 10 minutes. Allow tea to cool to room temperature, keeping it covered to retain the volatile oils. Strain the mixture through a small sieve lined with a coffee filter or cheese-cloth and stir in the vodka, if using. Use as you would a commercial mouthwash: swish it around in your mouth for about 1 minute, then spit it out.

Herb Fact

The thyme plant's essential oil, thymol, is an important ingredient in the commercial mouthwash Listerine.

SPICY CINNAMON MOUTHWASH

½ cup (62 g) ground cinnamon
1½ cups (350 ml) cider vinegar

Cinnamon's many healing properties include antimicrobial activity; cider vinegar is mildly acidic, so it is able to help flush your mouth of odor-causing bacteria. Combine the cinnamon and vinegar in a wide-mouth glass bottle with a tight-fitting lid (a large jelly jar works great). Store in a cool, dark place for approximately 2 weeks. Shake the jar gently every day or two so that contents don't settle. After the 2 weeks have passed, strain the mixture through a small sieve lined with a coffee filter or cheesecloth. Use as you would a commercial mouthwash: swish it around in your mouth for about 1 minute, then spit it out.

BREATH-FRIENDLY HERBAL CHEW

¼ cup (27 g) anise seed
¼ cup (12 g) cardamom pods

A dried seed mixture known as *mukhwas*, typically made by mixing anise seed and cardamom, is traditionally served after an Indian meal. It has a delicate licorice flavor (thanks to the anise) and is thought to aid digestion and lessen bad breath. Mix the spices together and store in a cool, dry place. To use, place a tablespoon (15 ml) of the mixture in your mouth and allow your saliva to soften the seeds slightly. Chew until the mixture begins to lose its flavor. Do not swallow the seed hulls.

MINT-PARSLEY MOUTHWASH

½ cup (120 ml) water
2 tablespoons (30 ml) fresh mint, coarsely chopped
2 tablespoons (30 ml) fresh parsley, coarsely chopped

Fresh parsley contains a high level of chlorophyll, a key ingredient in many natural breath-freshening products. And mint provides the classic scent we typically associate with dental care. Bring the water to a gentle boil. Steep the parsley and mint leaves in the water for 30 minutes. Allow tea to cool to room temperature, keeping it covered to retain the volatile oils. Strain the mixture through a small sieve lined with a coffee filter or cheesecloth. Use as you would a commercial mouthwash: swish it around in your mouth for about 1 minute, then spit it out.

Parsley

Parsley

A BRIEF HISTORY

Often relegated to the role of simple garnish, parsley actually has a long-standing reputation as a healing herb, with many practical applications for personal wellness. It's native to the Mediterranean region, where it has been grown for more than 2,500 years. The ancient Greek physician Dioscorides recommended parsley as a diuretic. It was worn by ancient Greek athletes who won contests and used to embellish tombs. The ancient Roman botanist known as Pliny the Elder mentioned it in his *Natural History* as an ingredient in sauces.

Parsley not only has a fresh flavor, but also contains volatile oils and antioxidants that can help freshen your breath. It may also give your immune system a good boost. Inserted into an ice pack, parsley can help ease the discomfort of a fresh bruise.

MAKING IT WORK FOR YOU

Parsley is available year-round in most grocery stores, and it is relatively inexpensive. Fresh parsley should be kept in the refrigerator in a plastic bag. If the parsley is slightly wilted, either sprinkle it lightly with some water or wash it without completely drying it before storing in the refrigerator. If you decide to grow your own, you will need to plant it only once, starting from seed. Parsley will return to your garden year after year once it is established. It grows best in moist, well-drained soil, with full sun.

CHAMOMILE CANKER-SORE RELIEF

1 cup (240 ml) water

2 teaspoons (10 ml) dried chamomile or 1 chamomile tea bag

Herbal experts often recommend chamomile to soothe inflammation, especially in mucous membrane areas such as the inside of the mouth. Bring the water to a gentle boil. Steep the chamomile in the water for 10 minutes. Strain and allow tea to cool to room temperature, keeping it covered to retain the volatile oils. Swish it around in your mouth for about 1 minute. Chamomile tea is quite drinkable, so no need to spit it out if you enjoy the taste. If you use a tea bag, extend the power of the tea by placing the used bag against the sore and holding it in place with your cheek or tongue for 10 to 20 minutes.

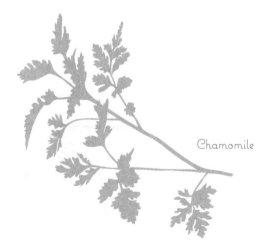

Chamomile

Chamomile

A BRIEF HISTORY

Considered by natural-healing experts to be an all-purpose herb that can relieve a variety of skin and digestive ailments, chamomile is a member of the aster family and native to Europe. Two varieties, German chamomile and Roman chamomile, are the most popular. If you are allergic to ragweed, you may want to avoid chamomile, a close relative.

As a tea, chamomile has been valued for thousands of years for its ability to ease muscle spasms and soothe the digestive tract. It is also well regarded as an effective and safe sleep aid. When applied topically, it can ease minor skin irritations—everything from bug bites and stings to mild burns. Studies show that the compounds in chamomile have antibacterial, antispasmodic, and anti-inflammatory effects.

MAKING IT WORK FOR YOU

German chamomile is a hardy annual with fernlike leaves that can pop up year after year if it is planted in a sunny spot and allowed to reseed. Roman chamomile, on the other hand, is technically a perennial with coarser leaves that grow lower to the ground. If you are planting either type, it is best to buy plants that have not yet begun to flower, because the plant will have more energy to put toward healthy root development.

TEA-TREE OIL MOUTH RINSE

2 to 3 drops tea-tree essential oil
1 cup (240 ml) water

While the exact cause of most canker sores is unknown, citrus or acidic foods, such as lemons, oranges, pineapples, apples, figs, tomatoes, and strawberries, can send your pain levels skyrocketing, so steer clear of them. In the meantime, try this simple tea-tree mouth rinse. The volatile oils possess antiseptic qualities that may help bring relief. Mix the oil with the water. Use as you would a commercial mouthwash: swish it around in your mouth for about 1 minute, then spit it out.

Herb Fact

Tea-tree oil is extracted from the leaves of the tea tree (*Melaleuca alternifolia*), which is native to Australia.

SAGE TEA GARGLE

1 cup (240 ml) water
2 teaspoons (10 ml) dried sage

For most people, the pain from a canker sore only lasts a few days, and the sores usually heal on their own within a week or two. But if you're not the patient type, try this easy herbal rinse. Sage contains tannins, which herbal experts say have antiseptic qualities that can help send painful canker sores packing faster. Bring the water to a gentle boil. Steep the sage in the water for 10 minutes. Strain and allow tea to cool to room temperature, keeping it covered to retain the volatile oils. Use as you would a commercial mouthwash: swish it around in your mouth for about 1 minute, then spit it out.

HOMEMADE MINTY TOOTHPASTE

2 tablespoons (30 ml) baking soda

2 tablespoons (30 ml) vegetable glycerin

1/4 teaspoon (1 ml) table salt, preferably not coarse or kosher

10 drops peppermint or spearmint essential oil

If you have been working with some of the other formulas in this book, odds are you already have everything on hand to whip up a batch of minty-fresh toothpaste if you're in a pinch. It will see you through for a few days until you can restock your normal toothpaste. Combine the baking soda, glycerin, salt, and essential oil in a small bowl. Stir until mixture is smooth and similar in consistency to commercial toothpaste. Keep covered and use within 3 days.

CLOVE TOOTHACHE REMEDY

1 to 2 drops clove essential oil

Clove oil has a long-standing reputation as a folk remedy; recent studies show it has analgesic and antibacterial properties, making it an excellent remedy for temporary relief of toothache pain. Oil of clove contains 60 to 90 percent eugenol, which is an antimicrobial compound and also plays a role in deadening pain. Apply the oil with either a cotton swab or clean finger directly on the affected tooth, taking care to avoid the gums as much as possible.

GOLDENSEAL PASTE FOR GINGIVITIS

1 tablespoon (15 ml) goldenseal powder
1/2 teaspoon (3 ml) water

Gingivitis, or swollen, inflamed gums caused by tartar (the buildup of plaque along the gumline), is a leading culprit in periodontitis. Good oral hygiene is the way to prevent this buildup. If you want to enlist an herbal ally in your fight against gingivitis, experts say goldenseal can help in reducing inflammation. Combine the powder and water in the palm of your hand. Add a few extra drops of water, if necessary, until mixture is the same consistency as toothpaste. Spread onto a wet toothbrush and brush as usual. Goldenseal is a bitter-tasting herb, so you may want to follow up with a minty mouth rinse (see Mint-Parsley Mouthwash, page 34).

Clove

A BRIEF HISTORY

Cloves are the dried flower buds of the clove tree. They are known for their strong aroma and taste. In ancient China during the Han dynasty, it was necessary for anyone who spoke with the emperor directly to hold cloves in his mouth while doing so to mask the odor of his breath. This herb arrived in Europe before the first century CE, where it became increasingly popular in cooking and in healing; it was recommended as a treatment for upset stomach, gas, and a variety of other stomach complaints, as well as infertility, warts, and wounds.

The essential oil of clove has as its main component the substance eugenol, long considered an effective (though temporary) remedy for toothache pain, making it a staple in dentistry. Recent studies have proven its analgesic effects.

MAKING IT WORK FOR YOU

Clove trees grow in tropical climates, but the spice is readily available in whole and ground forms in grocery stores. Clove trees are native to a group of Indonesian islands once known as the Spice Islands. Store your cloves in a glass container with a tight lid in a cool, dark spot. Whole cloves can keep for a year, while ground cloves are good for three months.

EUCALYPTUS CHAPPED-LIP SALVE

¼ cup (60 ml) castor oil
10 drops eucalyptus essential oil

When winter rolls around, chapped lips are an all-too-common problem for most people. For natural relief, consider keeping a small jar of herb-enhanced castor oil at the ready. Place the castor oil in a small, tinted bottle with a tight lid (if you have an empty bottle with an eyedropper-style lid, it will work even better). Add the eucalyptus oil, seal the bottle, then shake vigorously to combine. Place a drop or two of the oil on your finger and rub gently onto your chapped lips for instant, soothing relief.

TOOTH-BOLSTERING GREEN TEA BLEND

4 cups (950 ml) water
2 tablespoons (30 ml) dried green tea
½ cup (12 g) fresh mint leaves

Did you know that green tea is a natural source of fluoride? While too much fluoride can be toxic, dentists have long found a small amount of fluoride to be an important ally in the fight against tooth decay. And with this particular blend of green tea, you also get the fresh-breath benefit of mint. Make a batch at night, and you'll have enough to sip throughout the day. Bring the water to a gentle boil and pour over the green tea and mint. Let mixture steep for about 10 minutes, keeping the cup covered to preserve the volatile oils. Strain, then refrigerate until ready to drink.

Herb Fact

All tea comes from the plant *Camellia sinensis*. Green tea is unfermented, while black tea undergoes fermentation.

Cold and Allergy Appeasers

FOR SOME, ALLERGY SEASON BRINGS A STEADY DRIP OR A NAGGING COUGH.
For others, cold weather or the beginning of the school year means a season of sniffles and hacking. No matter what causes cold or allergy symptoms to strike, however, you don't need to be miserable. Herbs can lessen the severity of many annoying cold and allergy symptoms, and in some cases, they may even help keep them at bay due to their antiviral properties.

The common cold is a viral infection that can be set in motion by over two hundred different viruses. Symptoms are usually mild and limited to sore throat and nasal congestion, occasionally with coughing. Seasonal flu, on the other hand, usually has more severe symptoms—fever, body aches, sore throat, cough, and congestion—that set in rapidly. Though there is no known cure for either, you can ease your suffering.

In this section, you will find a number of herbal mixtures to help allay bothersome cold and allergy symptoms. Herbal remedies are ideal for lessening congestion, opening stuffy nasal passages, calming coughs, and soothing irritated throats, all without the side effects typical of many over-the-counter drugs.

In any case, prevention really is the best medicine when it comes to cold and flu season. Practice good old-fashioned hand washing throughout the day and avoid touching your face, especially the eyes and nose, whenever possible. And, of course, keep communal surfaces clean. For household cleaning tips, check out the Your Herbal Home section starting on page 123.

If cold and flu symptoms persist for longer than a week to ten days, see a doctor to determine if a bacterial infection or allergies may be at play. Should a fever develop, also see your doctor; a sore throat accompanied by a fever can be a sign of a strep infection, which requires medical attention.

THROAT-SOOTHING LOZENGES

¹/₃ cup (80 ml) water

1 teaspoon (5 ml) dried licorice root, chopped

2 to 3 tablespoons (30 to 45 ml) honey

¹/₂ cup (60 g) slippery elm powder, plus extra to prevent sticking

Instead of loading up on expensive natural lozenges at the health-food store, make your own. Flavored with a hint of licorice and honey, these lozenges create a slick texture as they dissolve in your mouth, making them the perfect herbal remedy to coat and soothe a sore throat. Bring the water to a gentle boil. Steep the licorice in the water for 10 minutes. Pour the desired amount of honey (more or less, depending on your sweet tooth) into the bottom of a glass measuring cup. Strain the tea over the honey until the mixture measures ¹/₄ cup (60 ml). Stir until combined, then pour over ¹/₂ cup slippery elm powder. Stir until mixture forms stiff dough. Scatter a little extra slippery elm powder on a clean work surface and roll out the dough to about ¹/₄ inch (6 mm) thickness. Use the top of a very small bottle to cut the dough into small discs. Arrange on a small plate and let sit uncovered for 24 to 48 hours, or until thoroughly dry. Store in a cool, dark place and take as needed to relieve a sore throat.

Herb Fact

Amid the treasures in King Tut's tomb, archaeologists found licorice sticks.

KICK-THAT-SORE-THROAT TEA

1 cup (240 ml) water

¼ teaspoon (1 ml) ground cayenne pepper

2 teaspoons (10 ml) honey

Juice from ½ lemon

Sometimes you just want to give a sore throat a kick in the pants, and this spicy drink concoction is likely to do the trick. The small dose of cayenne pepper will assist in clearing your sinuses, and the lemon provides an extra hit of vitamin C. Naturally, don't try this formula if you are averse to peppers. Bring water to a boil and stir in the cayenne pepper. Let sit for about 5 minutes, then stir in the honey and lemon juice. Let cool to a comfortable temperature before drinking.

Herb Fact

Though Cayenne is the capital of French Guiana, only a tiny fraction of the spicy fruit of the capsicum plant comes from there. The American Spice Trade Association considers the name "cayenne pepper" a misnomer and urges people to call this herb "red pepper."

ANISE SEED EXPECTORANT TEA

1 teaspoon (5 ml) anise seed

1 cup (240 ml) water

1 teaspoon (5 ml) honey, optional

Expectorants are compounds that help thin mucous, allowing the body to cough more productively. Expectorants are found in many over-the-counter cold relievers, but if you'd like to try a natural alternative, experts advise turning to anise seed. Put the anise seeds in a shallow bowl and crush slightly by firmly pressing down on the seeds with the back of a spoon. Bring water to a gentle boil. Transfer seeds to a cup and steep the seeds in the water for 10 minutes. If you find the licorice flavor to be bitter, sweeten with a bit of honey.

Anise

COUGH-CLEANSING THROAT RINSE

1 cup (240 ml) water

1 teaspoon (5 ml) dried sage or dried thyme

1/2 teaspoon (3 ml) salt, optional

If you have a wet cough that's irritating your throat, try this tea that may help clear the congestion. Bring water to a gentle boil. Steep the sage or thyme in the water for 10 minutes. Strain and allow tea to cool to a comfortable temperature, keeping it covered to retain the volatile oils. Add salt, if desired, and stir until dissolved. Gargle to clear your throat of mucous and reduce inflammation.

CINNAMON SORE-THROAT MILK

1 cup (240 ml) milk

1/2 teaspoon (3 ml) cinnamon

1/2 teaspoon (3 ml) powdered ginger

1 tablespoon (15 ml) of honey

If a hacking cough or sore throat has you wide awake and miserable before bedtime, a warm cup of cinnamon milk just might help you get a restful night's sleep. Stir the cinnamon and ginger into the milk and heat in the microwave or on the stovetop until warm. Stir in the honey until dissolved. Serve warm.

Cinnamon

A BRIEF HISTORY

As one of the first spices to be traded among ancient cultures, cinnamon was once considered as precious as gold. The Chinese used it as a treatment for fever and diarrhea, as did Indian healers in the Ayurvedic tradition. The Egyptians added it to their embalming formulas. Given its warm and inviting aroma, it's no wonder the Greeks and Romans used cinnamon as both a perfume and an indigestion remedy.

While most people consider cinnamon an essential kitchen spice, it also has a number of uses in aiding digestion and fighting infection. Studies show that cinnamon has anti-inflammatory and antimicrobial properties. And, perhaps because of all the wonderful memories of baked goods we associate with cinnamon, a drop or two of its essential oil is a key ingredient in many housewarming aromatherapy formulas.

MAKING IT WORK FOR YOU

While there are more than a hundred varieties of this aromatic tree, most commercial cinnamon comes from two main types. Ceylon cinnamon, native to Sri Lanka, but also produced in India, the Caribbean, and Brazil, has a lighter, sweeter, and more delicate flavor. Cassia tree cinnamon, which comes from Southeast Asia and is produced in Indonesia, Burma, China, and Vietnam, tends to be less expensive. Both are available in stick and powdered form.

HOREHOUND COUGH SYRUP

2 cups (475 ml) water

2 tablespoons (30 ml) fresh or dried horehound honey

This old-fashioned elixir relies on a very sweet ingredient, honey, to render it into a delicious, smooth syrup. Keep a bottle handy to coat the throat and quell an irritating cough. Bring the water to a gentle boil. Steep the horehound in the water for about 10 minutes. Strain the tea and measure the amount of liquid that remains. Transfer to a large glass bottle and add an equal amount of honey as there is liquid. Shake well until mixture is thoroughly combined. Cover and refrigerate. Take a spoonful at a time, up to 4 times a day.

EUCALYPTUS OR PEPPERMINT LARYNGITIS STEAM REMEDY

3 cups (700 ml) water

1/4 teaspoon (1 ml) eucalyptus or peppermint essential oil

When a virus or too much talking robs you of your voice, a little steam laced with an essential oil can help restore things to normal. Eucalyptus contains a chemical called cineole that helps to fight infection and to relieve throat inflammation, and peppermint possesses many anti-bacterial properties, while warm steam soothes and moisturizes dry, irritated tissues. Bring water to a simmer in a small pot, remove from heat, and add the essential oil of your choice. Sit down at a table, placing the pot in front of you on a heatproof trivet. Position your face over the pot at a distance so that the steam doesn't burn your face and drape a towel over the back of your head to form a mini-sauna. Breathe in the steam for 10 to 15 minutes, pausing for fresh air as needed. Repeat 3 times a day.

LEMON VERBENA SINUS STEAM REMEDY

3 cups (700 ml) water
10 drops lemon verbena essential oil

Sinus pain is often the unwelcome tagalong during allergy season, and the distinct, dense headache pressure it brings can be highly uncomfortable. Fortunately, the bright, gentle scent of lemon verbena can help unblock your congested passages and provide some relief. Bring water to a simmer in a small pot, remove from heat, and add the essential oil. Sit down at a table, placing the pot in front of you on a heatproof trivet. Position your face over the pot at a distance so that the steam doesn't burn your face and drape a towel over the back of your head to form a mini-sauna. Breathe in the steam for 10 to 15 minutes, pausing for fresh air as needed. Repeat 3 times a day.

ANTIVIRAL GINGER TEA

1 cup (240 ml) water

1 tablespoon (15 ml) fresh, grated ginger

1 teaspoon (5 ml) honey, optional

In both Ayurvedic and traditional Chinese medicine, ginger is considered one of the most versatile herbs for treating colds. Scientists have even isolated several chemicals in ginger that may play a role in fighting cold viruses, or rhinoviruses. Other compounds in ginger have been shown to help reduce pain and fever, suppress coughing, and provide a mild sedative effect that helps you rest. Bring the water to a gentle boil. Steep the ginger in the water for 10 to 15 minutes. Strain the tea and stir in the honey, if desired, then drink.

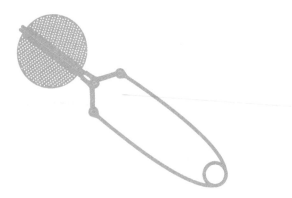

Ginger

A BRIEF HISTORY

The ancient Greeks added ginger to specialty breads (an early version of gingerbread), but after the fall of the Roman Empire, this gnarled, bumpy root with the strong, spicy flavor had almost disappeared from use throughout Europe, until the famed explorer Marco Polo rediscovered ginger on his trip through Asia. Today, though its popularity is firmly rooted in a variety of cuisines, most ginger comes from India.

A long-time home remedy for motion sickness, ginger tea has been praised for helping to relieve both dizziness and nausea. Clinical studies show that it is indeed effective against nausea and vomiting. It also relieves digestive spasms. Additionally, ginger may help fight colds because of its antiviral properties and sinus-clearing heat.

MAKING IT WORK FOR YOU

Ginger is a tropical plant, so if you want to grow it yourself, you'll probably need a greenhouse. Since it is widely available in grocery stores, it is far easier to buy fresh. To prepare fresh ginger, simply peel or scrape away the thin outer skin and grate or thinly slice into pieces. If you don't plan on using a large amount all at once, wrap whole pieces in a resealable plastic bag and store in the freezer. Pull it out of the freezer when needed and use a grater to get the amount you desire.

COLD-FIGHTING ONION REMEDY

2 to 3 thick slices sweet onion, such as Vidalia

2 tablespoons (30 ml) honey

Biologically speaking, the onion is a close relative to garlic and contains many similar antiviral compounds that may help prevent a cold or clear it up faster. As a medicinal plant, it has a long and storied history, from ancient Greece and Rome to India. The simple sugar in the honey helps draw the juice out of the onion slices. Place the onion slices in a glass bowl and drizzle with the honey, turning the slices to make sure they are well coated. Cover the bowl and let sit at room temperature for 3 to 4 hours. Drain the juice that collects and take by the spoonful to relieve sinus congestion.

Herb Fact

Onions have been cultivated for more than 5,000 years. The ancient Egyptians revered the onion, evidence of which has been found in royal tombs, while the ancient Greeks and Romans attributed a number of health benefits to onions.

SNIFFLE-STOPPING TEA

1 cup (240 ml) water

2 tablespoons (30 ml) fresh watercress

Since ancient times, watercress has been credited with many uses. Records from Pliny the Elder indicate that the early Romans believed watercress had more than forty medicinal and practical uses, including the ability to drive away snakes and neutralize scorpion venom. While your own needs may be less dire, as your cold runs its course, modern herbal wisdom suggests a cup of watercress tea might relieve your sniffles for a while. Bring the water to a gentle boil and pour over the watercress. Let steep for 10 to 15 minutes. Strain, then drink when tea has reached a comfortable temperature.

Stomach Soothers

HERBAL REMEDIES FOR THE STOMACH HAVE A LONG HISTORY IN BOTH THE NEW WORLD AND THE OLD–almost as long a history as humans have with stomach ailments! From treating minor complaints such as a sour stomach to more serious discomforts such as ulcers or parasites, herbal lore yields many historical remedies. Pliny the Elder noted the soothing effect of mint on the upset stomach; some Native American peoples used dandelion to treat indigestion, and the plant artemisia was commonly known as "wormwood" due to its ability to help sufferers afflicted with parasites. Today, whether it is an ill-timed bout of flatulence, a painful episode of post-holiday heartburn, or the nausea that accompanies a brief illness, digestive irritation strikes everyone. But before we get to the herbal remedies that may bring some relief, it is important to be clear about those situations that experts say shouldn't go unexamined.

Heartburn is a painful burning sensation in the chest commonly caused when stomach acid flows up instead of down. Beyond overeating and spicy foods, common triggers include stress, smoking, and the use of some over-the-counter pain relievers. If you experience heartburn several times a week, it is important that you see your doctor, as you may be suffering from a more serious condition; likewise, any other gastrointestinal ailment that doesn't respond to a few days of home remedies or is accompanied by fever, severe pain, or dramatic weight loss warrants follow-up with your doctor.

That said, generations of people have relied upon a number of frontline herbal remedies to relieve their most common stomach ailments. While there are as yet few formal scientific studies to establish their effectiveness, thousands of years of anecdotal reports indicate helpfulness—so why not see if some of these trusted formulas work for you?

Dandelion

CHAMOMILE HEARTBURN RELIEVER

1 cup (240 ml) water

1 tablespoon (15 ml) whole dried chamomile flowers

1 teaspoon (5 ml) honey, optional

Chamomile's benefits as an after-dinner beverage are well-known. Not only does it have a pleasing aroma and delicious flavor, but it also, according to herbal experts, soothes an irritated digestive tract. In terms of heartburn relief, chamomile helps relieve the inflamed membranes and "quench the fire," so to speak. Bring the water to a gentle boil. Steep the chamomile in the water for 10 to 15 minutes, keeping the mixture covered to preserve the volatile oils. Strain the tea and add honey, if desired, then drink.

Herb Fact

In *The Tale of Peter Rabbit*, written by Beatrix Potter in 1902, it is chamomile tea that Peter is given by his mother after he overeats in Mr. McGregor's garden.

SLIPPERY ELM HEARTBURN TEA

1 cup (240 ml) water

2 teaspoons (10 ml) slippery elm powder

Long used by Native Americans to treat discomforts ranging from sore throats to heartburn, this powdered herb, when mixed with water, takes on a slick, gel-like texture that seems to have a natural ability to coat and soothe irritated tissues. As a tea, slippery elm has a very faint flavor and a mild maple scent. Bring the water to a gentle boil, then stir in the slippery elm powder. Let sit for 10 to 15 minutes until tea reaches a comfortable temperature for drinking.

Herb Fact

Before the invention of refrigeration, slippery elm bark was used to preserve meat—the bark was soaked in water, then wrapped around the meat to retard spoilage.

Slippery Elm

DILL-SEED INDIGESTION TEA

1 tablespoon (15 ml) dill seeds

1 cup (240 ml) water

1 teaspoon (5 ml) honey, optional

Eating pickles after a meal is a long-standing folk remedy for avoiding heartburn. Though it runs counter to the conventional wisdom, some say the acidity of the pickles actually helps balance the pH levels in your stomach. Herbalists, on the other hand, are more likely to point to the power of dill. If you're not a fan of eating pickles, then this herbal antidote may be worth a try. Place the dill seeds in a shallow bowl and crush slightly by firmly pressing down on the seeds with the back of a spoon. Transfer seeds to a cup and bring the water to a gentle boil. Steep the seeds in the water for 20 to 30 minutes. Strain and add honey, if desired, then drink.

Dill

Dill is mentioned in the Ebers Papyrus (approximately 1500 BCE); the ancient Egyptians used it to relieve headaches. Stems of dill were found in the tomb of Amenhotep II. To the ancient Greeks and Romans, dill symbolized wealth and luck. Dried seed heads were hung in the home, over doorways and above cradles, to symbolize love and protection.

Apparently native to Europe and Asia, dill also became featured in many cuisines. Along the way, people figured out that dill has some beneficial health effects, too. According to some food historians, the Holy Roman emperor Charlemagne was fond of having his banquet tables strewn with dill so that overindulgent guests could use it to settle any digestive upsets. Later, early American colonists referred to dill seeds as "meeting house seeds," as they were chewed during long church services to keep hunger pangs at bay. Today, studies show that dill's compounds, including monoterpenes and flavonoids, may have antibacterial, and antioxidant effects.

In home remedies, dill is most often consumed as a tea to help settle an upset stomach or ensure a good night's sleep. The seeds are stronger and more flavorful than the leaves, though both can be used. In cooking, dill is of course most commonly associated with pickling, though dill is a welcome addition to many other dishes, as well.

In terms of storage, fresh dill has a short shelf life, so your best bet is to grow your own if you enjoy the taste in cooking. Fortunately, it is very easy to start a dill patch in most climates. Just make sure you have a sunny spot and ample space for the roots to grow deep. Dill plants are tall, so you may want them toward the back of a bed or container. Harvest leaves before the plants reach full flower. Use fresh dill sprigs immediately. In autumn, collect the seeds after they turn brown, then allow them to air-dry on a tray. Store seeds in a cool, dark place for six months. Leave a few plants alone, so they drop their seeds on the ground to produce a nice patch the next year.

Dill

NATURAL GINGER ALE FOR NAUSEA

½ cup (48 g) sliced ginger

2 cups (475 ml) water

½ cup (120 ml) honey

2 cups (475 ml) club soda

Ginger is a true powerhouse when it comes to digestive problems; it can settle upset stomachs and diminish cramps and gas pains, but its reputation largely stands upon its ability to quell nausea symptoms. Some scientific studies even suggest it may work better in fighting motion sickness than the active ingredient in many over-the-counter medications. Combine the ginger and water in a small saucepan and bring to a simmer. Let simmer for 5 minutes, remove from heat, then let sit for another 20 minutes. Add the honey while the mixture is warm and stir until dissolved. Strain to remove the ginger pieces and refrigerate mixture until cool. Combine equal amounts of ginger mixture and club soda over ice. Stir and enjoy.

Herb Fact

A chunk of ginger that you buy fresh from the grocery store is called a "hand."

LEMON MINT TEA FOR GAS

1 cup (240 ml) water
2 teaspoons (10 ml) dried lemon mint

While both mint tea and juice of lemons are popular ingredients in many of the home remedies in this book, this tea is made from the lemon mint plant. This herb has a distinct lemony odor when crushed, and the tea is often described as having a lemonade-like flavor. Herbal experts say it can relieve the cramps associated with gas pains, and may also ease nausea. Bring the water to a gentle boil. Steep the lemon mint in the water for 10 to 15 minutes. Strain the tea and let cool to desired temperature, then drink.

Herb Fact

Lemon mint's scientific name, *Monarda citriodora*, refers to the lemony scent of its leaves. Native to North America, this plant was used by the Hopi, as well as other Native American peoples, for flavoring food, for making tea, and as an insect repellant.

OLD-FASHIONED ITALIAN NAUSEA TEA

1 cup (240 ml) water

3 to 4 whole fresh basil leaves

1 teaspoon (5 ml) honey, optional

Herbal experts point to basil, a member of the mint family, as having the power to relieve all kinds of stomach upsets, including nausea and acid reflux. But you don't have to make a big batch of pesto sauce to see if it works for you. A simple cup of tea will do nicely. Bring the water to a gentle boil. Steep the basil leaves in the water for 10 to 15 minutes, keeping it covered to preserve the volatile oils. Strain the tea and add honey, if desired, then drink.

Herb Fact

The variety known as Holy Basil, or tulsi, is said to be sacred to the Hindu god Vishnu.

Basil

Basil

Basil is a fast-growing herb with a number of popular varieties, including sweet basil (most often used in Italian cooking), Thai basil, and lemon basil. Not surprisingly, many cultures, from India and Southeast Asia to the Mediterranean, have held basil in high regard through the years. Indeed, the name "basil" is derived from an old Greek word, *basilikon*, which means "royal."

Studies show that basil's constituents have antibacterial and anti-inflammatory effects. A member of the mint family, basil is a highly fragrant plant with many culinary uses. As a home remedy it can be used to ease nausea and acid reflux. And theoretically, since both herbs share similar volatile compounds and antibacterial properties, you could substitute basil for mint in many of the cleaning formulas in the latter section of this book.

MAKING IT WORK FOR YOU

Although basil grows best outdoors and is easy to start from seed, it is also relatively effortless to grow indoors, if you place its container on a sunny south-facing windowsill away from any drafts. In the normal life cycle of the plant, leaf production slows down considerably once flowers start to bloom in late summer, so take care to pinch off any flower stems to keep the plant producing its tasty leaves as long as possible.

ALL-NATURAL CONSTIPATION RELIEVER

½ cup (61 g) rhubarb, chopped

¼ cup (60 ml) water

2 to 3 tablespoons (30 to 45 ml) honey

Greek yogurt, optional

Here's a wonderful way to balance your system. While the leaves of the rhubarb plant are poisonous and should never be eaten, consuming the stalk portion of the plant can supply your system with anthraquinone compounds, natural stimulant laxatives. Rhubarb also contains high levels of tannins and pectin, which help reduce inflammation in the colon and keep the laxative effect in check. Limit yourself to 1 serving; rhubarb is not appropriate for people with certain health conditions, so refer to the safe-use guidelines on page 204. Combine the rhubarb and water in a small saucepan and bring to a simmer. Let simmer for 10 to 15 minutes until the water is absorbed and the fruit is soft. Remove from heat and stir in the honey until mixture reaches desired sweetness. Either cool to room temperature or serve warm. A dollop of Greek yogurt may be served on top, if desired.

Herb Fact

In British East Africa, between World Wars I and II, physicians relied on rhubarb to treat bacterial dysentery, a common and often fatal disease.

RASPBERRY LEAF-GINGER STOMACH SOOTHER

2 teaspoons (10 ml) dried raspberry leaf tea

1 teaspoon (5 ml) fresh, grated ginger

1 cup (240 ml) water

1 teaspoon (5 ml) honey, optional

If your upset stomach is related to diarrhea, it is important to make sure you're getting plenty of fluids. Raspberry leaf tea is an age-old remedy for gastrointestinal problems that cause trouble at that end of the tract. The high tannin content of the leaves helps soothe inflammation, and ginger, another anti-inflammatory, has long been used as a remedy for fighting nausea. Bring the water to a gentle boil. Steep raspberry leaf tea and ginger in the water for 10 minutes. Strain and add honey, if desired, then drink.

Ginger

Stress Relievers

STRESS IS AN UNFORTUNATE FACT OF LIFE–whether it stems from the pressures of work or the demands of modern life, it tends to be a recurring issue for many people. Specific health issues, including headaches, muscle tension, and insomnia, are commonly associated with stress. Relaxation is recommended, but hard to achieve. However, nature has long provided its own solutions: herbs. There are many herbs with relaxing and rejuvenating properties. Additionally, the act of preparing herbal remedies can be calming–think of the soothing quality of preparing a cup of tea or running a bath. In these multiple ways, herbs can have restorative and stress-relieving effects.

The painful throbbing feeling of a tension headache is so common that, according to the National Headache Foundation in the United States, close to 80 percent of the general population will experience a tension-type headache at some point in their lives. These headaches are often triggered by stress, anxiety, fatigue, or anger; fortunately, three out of four of these things may be relieved in part by herbal remedies.

According to research at the U.S. National Institutes of Health, about 30 to 40 percent of adults say they experience some insomnia over the course of a year. That lack of sleep can definitely have an impact on your day-to-day life. The good news is that a number of lifestyle changes can lead to more restful slumber, according to the sleep experts, including going to bed and getting up at a regular time through-out the week; avoiding alcohol, nicotine, and caffeine, especially before bedtime; and making sure your bedroom is appropriately comfortable (most people sleep better in a cool, dark room). In addition, herbal remedies can be very effective for the occasional night when you have difficulty falling asleep.

Remember, if these strategies don't work to relieve your symptoms, do follow up with your doctor. Like headaches, insomnia can be a symptom of an underlying health condition; and if left untreated, insomnia can lead to other health problems.

LEMON BALM BEDTIME TEA

1 cup (240 ml) water
2 teaspoons (10 ml) dried lemon balm
1 teaspoon (5 ml) dried chamomile
1 teaspoon (5 ml) honey, optional

Lemon balm is native to southern Europe and is commonly planted in gardens to attract bees. Herbal experts say that the volatile oils in lemon balm offer mild muscle relaxation, an aid in helping you sleep. Chamomile is also known for its relaxing effect. While the bright flavor of lemon balm can complement many other types of herbs, it pairs particularly well with chamomile, especially if slumber is your goal. Bring the water to a gentle boil. Steep the lemon balm and chamomile in the water for 10 to 15 minutes, keeping it covered to preserve the volatile oils. Strain the tea and add honey, if desired, then drink.

Lemon balm

HERBAL SLEEP SOAK

4 cups (480 g) powdered milk

2 cups (240 g) Epsom salt

2 cups (440 g) baking soda

¼ cup (60 ml) liquid castile soap

15 drops lavender essential oil

8 drops chamomile essential oil

1 teaspoon (5 ml) isopropyl alcohol

It is well known that the ancient Romans were adept at the art of relaxation, and they regularly tapped into the soothing power of herbs to aid their efforts, using lavender, in particular, to scent their public bath waters, perfumes, and soaps. Try forgetting about modern life for a while with your own herbal bedtime bath ritual. Combine the milk, Epsom salt, and baking soda in a large bowl and stir with a spoon or whisk until well combined. Add the soap, essential oils, and alcohol. Stir well for several minutes to incorporate all ingredients (the mixture will be somewhat gritty). Store in a covered container and add 1 cup (220 g) to a warm bath (a too-hot bath before bedtime may make getting to sleep even more difficult).

INSOMNIAC'S TEA

1 cup (240 ml) water

2 teaspoons (10 ml) dried chamomile

1 teaspoon (5 ml) dried passionflower

1 teaspoon (5 ml) honey, optional

For thousands of years, chamomile has been a mainstay ingredient in formulas for helping people feel more relaxed. And recent formal scientific research indicates this herb may also help ease anxiety symptoms. Though little research has been done on passionflower, the studies that do exist suggest that it also has antianxiety effects. So if you want to help maximize your odds for a restful night's sleep after an especially stressful day, try this tea before bedtime. Bring the water to a gentle boil. Steep the chamomile and passionflower in the water for 10 to 15 minutes, keeping it covered to preserve the volatile oils. Strain the tea and add honey, if desired, then drink.

Herb Fact

The passionflower was first documented by Spanish explorers who found it growing in Peru in 1569.

WILLOW BARK HEADACHE TEA

1 cup (240 ml) water

2 teaspoons (10 ml) dried willow bark

1 teaspoon (5 ml) honey, optional

Often referred to as "herbal aspirin," willow bark contains the aspirin-like compound salicin. Unlike regular aspirin, it is unlikely that a cup of willow bark tea will irritate your stomach; however, people who have been advised to avoid aspirin should also avoid willow bark. Bring the water to a gentle boil, add the willow bark, and simmer for about 10 minutes. Remove from heat and let steep for 30 more minutes, keeping it covered to preserve the volatile oils. Strain the tea and add honey, if desired, then drink.

Herb Fact

The ancient Greek physician Hippocrates advised patients suffering from pain to chew on willow bark.

Willow Bark

For thousands of years, herbalists have faithfully turned to willow bark for everything from clearing the complexion and stopping vomiting to suppressing sexual urges. While those uses remain questionable, willow bark's undeniable analgesic effect led to its becoming the precursor to one of the most well-known, over-the-counter pain relievers in modern medicine: aspirin. As early as 500 BCE, white willow bark was used by the Chinese to alleviate fever and pain. Later, the ancient Egyptians and Greeks employed it in a similar manner.

White willow bark is a natural source of salicylates, the active chemicals in aspirin, so it can be used in much the same way. That said, the same cautions apply to willow bark: it is not appropriate for children under the age of sixteen, and it should be avoided by people who are sensitive to aspirin or have chronic gastrointestinal conditions.

MAKING IT WORK FOR YOU

Today most commercial products are derived from the white willow tree. Willows grow quickly in moist gardens with full sun. They must be pruned regularly. If you want to try willow bark tea, buying it at a health-food store is by far the easiest option. The tea is very bitter, so add a spoonful of honey to make it more palatable.

CUCUMBER-MINT HEADACHE COMPRESS

1 cup (240 ml) water

2 teaspoons (10 ml) dried mint

2 to 4 slices fresh cucumber

According to herbal lore, the cooling combination of cucumber and mint can be an effective duo in silencing the pain of a pounding headache, especially if it is occurring behind the eyes. Bring the water to a gentle boil. Steep the mint in the water for 10 to 15 minutes, keeping it covered to preserve the volatile oils. Strain the tea and refrigerate until ready to use. If you don't have time to let the tea cool in the refrigerator, use half the amount of water and add ice cubes after straining to cool the tea faster. To use, dip a clean washcloth in the cold tea and squeeze until damp. Lie down in a comfortable spot and place 1 to 2 cucumber slices over each eye. Then position the damp compress over your eyes and forehead and rest quietly until the headache subsides.

Spearmint

LEMON BALM-LAVENDER HEADACHE SOAK

1 cup (240 ml) water
2 tablespoons (30 ml) dried lemon balm
2 tablespoons (30 ml) dried lavender

If your workday headache follows you home and threatens to ruin a good night's sleep, ease away the tension with this soothing bath remedy. Lemon balm and lavender are a dynamic aromatherapy combination that's often recommended for headache relief. Bring the water to a gentle boil, then pour over the lemon balm and lavender. Let mixture steep for about 10 minutes, keeping it covered to preserve the volatile oils. In the meantime, draw a warm bath. Strain the tea, add it to the bath, and enjoy a relaxing soak.

Herb Fact

In the Middle Ages, it was believed that a sprinkle of lavender-scented water on a lover's head would keep the person faithful.

LAVENDER-CHAMOMILE BATH SALTS

1 cup (120 g) Epsom salt

10 drops lavender essential oil

10 drops chamomile essential oil

For ultimate relaxation, nothing beats taking a bath. And you don't have to rely on store-bought bath salts when you have your own herbal supply chest to turn to. Lavender and chamomile are both well-known as calming herbs; together, they make a delightfully relaxing bath combination. Place the salt in a clear glass jar and add the essential oils. Cover with a lid and shake gently to distribute the oils. Add a handful (about ½ cup, or 60 g) to your bath and enjoy a little relaxing aromatherapy along with a skin-rejuvenating soak. Store in a cool, dark place when not in use.

Lavender

RELAXING LAVENDER-ROSE HIP BATH BOMB

1/4 cup (12 g) dried lavender

1/4 cup dried (30 g) rose hip

1 1/4 cup (275 g) baking soda

1/2 cup (100 g) citric acid powder

20 drops lavender essential oil

2 teaspoons (10 ml) cold water

1/3 cup (80 ml) almond oil

Turn your next bath into a floral-scented paradise with your own homemade bath bomb. The "secret ingredient" in this simple formula is citric acid. Naturally derived from citrus fruits and often used as a preservative, citric acid is sold in powdered form and easy to buy online. Coat an eight-cup muffin tin with a thin layer of almond oil and set aside. Using a food processor, grind the lavender and rose hip into a coarse powder. Combine the baking soda, citric acid powder, and lavender-rose hip powder in a large glass bowl. Add the essential oil and water. Stirring constantly, add the almond oil just until the mixture holds together. Divide the mixture among the cups of the muffin tin and cover with waxed paper. Use the bottom of a glass or back of a spoon to press the covered mixture firmly into the cups of the muffin tin. Let sit for 5 to 10 minutes, then gently tap to release the bombs onto the waxed paper. Let sit for 2 to 3 days until thoroughly dry. Once dry, store them in an airtight container until ready to use.

Rose

A BRIEF HISTORY

With a distinct, unforgettable fragrance, the highly prized rose has left a conspicuous floral trail throughout history. From the Egyptians, who prized rose petals as an air freshener and perfume, to the European herbalists, who used dried rose petal tea to treat conditions as diverse as headaches and tuberculosis, almost every culture that has come in contact with this fragrant flower has found some use for it.

Where medicinal uses are concerned, the beautiful, soft rose petal is not the true prize; rather, the rose hip, the central portion of the flower that remains after the petals fall away, is believed by many natural-healing experts to be a valuable source of vitamin C. Medicinal benefits aside, however, the wonderful scent of roses makes the petals a fitting addition to sachets, potpourri, and beauty products.

MAKING IT WORK FOR YOU

Roses have been bred for thousands of years to adapt to almost every climate, so visit a reliable nursery or garden center to figure out what variety will work best for your area. That said, keep in mind that older "heirloom" varieties are generally more fragrant than newer hybrids, but they often afford less dramatic blossoms and are faster to wilt.

ENERGIZING HEADACHE TEA

1 cup (240 ml) water
2 teaspoons (10 ml) dried green tea
2 teaspoons (10 ml) dried or fresh mint

Caffeine may help to relieve some types of headaches and is a common ingredient in many over-the-counter headache relief formulas. But everyone responds to caffeine differently, and too much caffeine in your system may also cause headaches. However, a cup of green tea has less caffeine than a cup of black tea, and a substantially lower amount than coffee. Bring the water to a gentle boil and pour over the green tea and mint. Let mixture steep for about 10 minutes, keeping covered to preserve the volatile oils. Strain, then drink when the tea reaches a comfortable temperature.

Herb Fact

Coffee is, perhaps, the world's most widely used herbal medicine. According to the International Coffee Organization, 1.6 million cups are drunk each day in pursuit of its active ingredient, caffeine.

STRESS-RELIEVING AROMATHERAPY MIX

½ cup (120 ml) distilled water

30 drops lavender essential oil

10 drops chamomile essential oil

No time for a massage? You can still enjoy the stress-reducing power of herbal aromatherapy in this quick-to-apply spritz. For best results, use distilled water. Place the distilled water in a small spray bottle (preferably a dark-colored bottle, but any type of travel-size atomizer will do). Add the lavender and chamomile essential oils and shake well to distribute them. Spray onto your pulse points—the inside of your wrists, the back of your neck—for maximum benefit. Store in a cool, dark place when not in use.

Herb Fact

In England, Roman chamomile is often cultivated as a ground cover for garden pathways. When the herb is stepped on, it releases a pleasant aroma.

STRESS-RELIEVING MASSAGE OIL

½ cup (60 ml) almond oil

24 drops lavender essential oil

6 drops chamomile essential oil

6 drops sandalwood essential oil

4 drops ylang-ylang essential oil

Who hasn't felt amazingly better and more relaxed after a luxurious massage? But did you know that you can enhance that feeling with some essential oils added to your regular massage oil? Aromatherapists find that the combination of lavender, chamomile, sandalwood, and ylang-ylang is especially good for inducing a state of calm. Best of all, it is remarkably easy to make on your own. Place the almond oil in a dark glass bottle. Add the lavender, chamomile, sandalwood, and ylang-ylang essential oils, then shake well. Cover and store in a cool, dark place when not in use.

Hair and Skin Care

THE USE OF HERBAL INGREDIENTS IN BEAUTY AND PERSONAL HYGIENE PRODUCTS DATES BACK TO ANTIQUITY–and for good reason. Herbs have been used effectively for thousands of years in the pursuit of beauty and to combat common hair and skin problems. The ancient Egyptians used kohl, which included herbal ingredients, to line their eyes. They were also expert perfumers, creating pomades that included aromatic herbs such as cinnamon. Olive oil, often scented with leaves and flowers, was used to soften the skin. In ancient Rome, where bathing was both a social and personal activity, herb-based bath products were common. In old Japan, camellia oil was a popular hair product.

Herbs have also been used to treat skin and hair problems for thousands of years. Ancient Chinese healers prescribed a rhubarb-based lotion for eczema. Hippocates himself may have tried a horseradish-and-cumin preparation to slow hair loss. By the seventeenth century, the herbalist Nicolas Culpeper was able to draw on many centuries of herbal lore to recommend solutions for dealing with specific skin and hair problems, including thyme for eliminating warts, and yarrow for preventing baldness.

The long history of herbs in skin and hair care has been well noted by the modern industry—herbal ingredients are often the main selling point in commercial products. But there is no reason you cannot make your own equally effective, earth-friendly, and nontoxic creams, salves, lotions, cleansers, and more.

This section takes a head-to-toe approach to herbal solutions for skin and hair care, and offers some herbal beauty tips as well.

As always, if you have a condition that doesn't respond to treatment, by all means see your doctor. The appearance of our hair and skin not only reflects our general health, but also can affect the way we feel about ourselves and impact the way we interact with others, so it is worth obtaining professional advice.

ROSEMARY-LAVENDER SHAMPOO

2 cups (475 ml) water

½ cup (7 g) fresh rosemary, chopped

½ cup (24 g) dried lavender

2 cups (475 ml) baby shampoo

This simple formula is appealing for its gentle cleansing action and fresh, natural scent. Because you are diluting the baby shampoo, this herbal version won't create the same amount of suds; it will leave your hair soft and clean without stripping it to the point of dryness. Bring the water to a gentle boil, add the rosemary, and simmer for about 10 minutes. Remove from heat, add the lavender, and let steep for 30 more minutes, keeping covered to preserve the volatile oils. Strain, then stir in the shampoo. Transfer to a plastic bottle and use daily, if you like.

Herb Fact

Londoners must have believed rosemary could protect them from the plague. In 1603, during an outbreak that would eventually claim the lives of 38,000 people, the demand for the fragrant herb was so high that the price increased from one shilling for an armful to six shillings for a handful. Need another price to compare that to? Later records from 1625 indicate that having eighteen gallons of good ale delivered to your door would cost about three shillings, and an entire "fat pig" could be purchased for one shilling.

ROSEMARY HAIR RINSE

1 cup (240 ml) water
3 tablespoons (10 g) dried rosemary
4 cups (950 ml) room-temperature water
1 tablespoon (15 ml) cider vinegar

Unless your hair is particularly oily, you might not need to shampoo every day. If you're fighting dandruff, however, it is worth considering a shampoo-alternative like this gentle herbal hair rinse for the days in between shampooing. Bring the cup (240 ml) of water to a gentle boil, add the rosemary, and simmer for about 10 minutes. Remove from heat and let steep for 30 more minutes, keeping it covered to preserve the volatile oils. Strain, then mix with the room-temperature water and the vinegar. To use, pour over hair and scalp. Repeat until hair and scalp are completely saturated. Gently massage your scalp with your fingertips, then towel dry.

Rosemary

DANDRUFF-FIGHTING TEA-TREE OIL SHAMPOO

1 cup (240 ml) liquid castile soap
½ cup (120 ml) water
1 teaspoon (5 ml) almond oil
1 tablespoon (15 ml) tea-tree essential oil

Tea-tree oil's dandruff-fighting powers are well-known, so it is often an ingredient in commercial hair care products. But did you know how easy it is to make your own tea-tree oil shampoo? Combine the soap, water, almond oil, and tea-tree oil in a squeezable plastic bottle and shake well to combine ingredients. Let settle, then use as regularly as you would a store-bought shampoo.

Herb Fact
Research is under way to determine whether tea-tree oil may be useful in the treatment of bacterial infections.

SOOTHING FENNEL EYE COMPRESSES

1 cup (240 ml) water
2 teaspoons (10 ml) fennel seeds

Allergies, salty foods, and oversleeping, among other things, can lead to fluid retention, appearing as puffy eyes. No matter the cause, these easy-to-make compresses can help reduce the puffiness. Bring the water to a gentle boil. Place the fennel seeds in a teacup and cover with the hot water. Cover and let steep for 30 minutes. Refrigerate the cup and its contents overnight, keeping it covered to retain the volatile oils, then strain. Tear a paper towel in half and fold each piece into a patch-size square. Soak the patches in the cooled tea. Lie down in a comfortable spot with your head on a pillow. Place one patch over each eye and relax for 15 minutes or so. Refrigerate unused tea for up to 4 days, if you want to repeat the treatment.

Herb Fact

Fennel is very attractive to the swallowtail butterfly, whose caterpillars feed on the leaves.

Fennel

A BRIEF HISTORY

The ancient Greeks believed that fennel steeped into a tea could help people lose weight. In fact, they called it *marathron*, which means "to grow thin." Ironically, all parts of the plant—bulb, stalk, leaves, and seeds—are edible and delicious when properly prepared, so its other reputation as an appetite stimulant is equally deserved. Because of its distinct flavor and aroma, fennel is also one of the primary ingredients in the distilled spirits ouzo and absinthe.

Fennel's use today is mostly limited to cooking and medicine, but given the herb's reputation for easing digestive problems, it is common in some cultures to enjoy either the seeds or a tea brewed from its leaves after dinner. Studies show that the compounds in fennel have anti-inflammatory, antioxidant, and immune-boosting properties.

MAKING IT WORK FOR YOU

Fresh fennel is widely available in most grocery stores and can easily be brewed into a tasty tea. If you enjoy gardening, it is an easy-to-grow perennial that does well in rich, moist soil. Just make sure to plant it away from cilantro; if that is growing nearby, your fennel will not bear seeds. Some gardeners suggest the following technique for encouraging a sweeter, milder flavor: once the stems are about an inch (2.5 cm) thick, build a little dirt hill around the base of the plant; harvest it about ten days later.

ALL-PURPOSE PIMPLE FIGHTER

1½ teaspoons (7 ml) tea-tree essential oil

2 tablespoons (30 ml) witch hazel

2 tablespoons (30 ml) rose water

Not only is tea-tree oil well regarded as a dandruff remedy, herbal experts also say it can fight acne due to its strong antibacterial properties. That said, applying straight tea-tree oil to the skin can prompt further irritation, so dilute it with witch hazel and rose water to make it gentler. Combine the tea-tree oil, witch hazel, and rose water in a small jar or bottle and shake well to combine. Apply directly to affected areas after morning and evening cleansing, then allow to air-dry. Store in a cool, dry place when not in use.

ROSEMARY-OATMEAL FACIAL SCRUB

¼ cup (22 g) oatmeal, not instant

2 tablespoons (30 ml) powdered milk

1 tablespoon (15 ml) fresh rosemary

Water, to make a paste

Looking for a natural way to achieve glowing skin? Whip up a batch of this easy facial scrub once a week, and you may soon have friends asking for your beauty secrets. Add the oats, milk, and rosemary to a food processor. Combine until oats are finely ground. To use, pour half of the mixture into the palm of your hand, then add enough lukewarm water to make a paste. Apply to clean face and neck. Massage gently with the tips of your fingers in light upward strokes. Rinse thoroughly and pat skin dry. Refrigerate remaining scrub and repeat in 3 to 4 days.

MOISTURIZING FACE WASH

1/4 cup (60 ml) aloe vera gel
1 teaspoon (5 ml) vitamin E oil
1 teaspoon (5 ml) glycerin
15 drops lavender essential oil

Dry skin, especially during the winter months, can make your face feel tight and prone to flakiness. Fortunately, this gentle herbal cleanser can help restore a smooth and supple finish to your skin. Combine the aloe vera gel, vitamin E oil, glycerin, and lavender essential oil in a small dark bottle with a lid. Before using, shake well to combine ingredients. Apply with cotton balls, taking care to avoid the eye area. Rinse with lukewarm water and pat skin dry with a soft cloth.

ALL-PURPOSE TONER

½ cup (24 g) dried chamomile
1 cup (240 ml) cider vinegar
1 tablespoon (15 ml) witch hazel
2 cups (475 ml) distilled water

Toners can help cleanse skin and tighten pores; however, some people find commercial toners to be too harsh. If you're looking for a gentle alternative, this formula might be right for you. Pack the chamomile into a pint-size glass jar with a tight-fitting lid. Add the cider vinegar, then cover tightly. Store in a cool, dark place for 3 to 6 weeks, taking care to shake the jar gently every few days to keep the contents active. Strain mixture, reserving the vinegar. Add the witch hazel to the vinegar and stir to combine. Transfer ¼ cup (60 ml) of the mixture to a plastic bottle with a tight-fitting lid and dilute by adding 2 cups (475 ml) of distilled water. Apply the toner to your freshly washed face and neck with cotton pads. Refrigerate the mixture when not in use. The toner will last about a year.

Chamomile

ALL-NATURAL WRINKLE PREVENTER

¼ cup (60 ml) wheat germ oil
40 drops calendula essential oil

Wheat germ oil is an important ingredient in many commercial facial moisturizers because it gives dry skin a soft and supple texture. Plus, it is an excellent source of vitamin E, which is believed to help fight signs of aging. The calendula essential oil helps promote the growth of new skin cells. Herbal experts say that the combination of these two ingredients can provide a gentle at-home alternative for great skin care. Combine the wheat germ and calendula oils in a small jar or bottle and shake well to combine. Apply a small amount to your face and throat after morning and evening cleansing. Store in a cool, dry place when not in use.

ALL-PURPOSE CUTICLE CONDITIONER

2 tablespoons (30 ml) castor oil
5 drops lavender essential oil

If you're prone to ragged, dry cuticles, turn to this easy-to-prepare cuticle conditioner. Castor oil is rich in vitamin E, which is very beneficial to your skin. Use faithfully every night, and you should see noticeable results within a few weeks. Combine the castor and lavender oils in a small glass jar and shake well to distribute. At night, dab a small amount on each cuticle and massage gently until oil is absorbed. Keep sealed and store in a cool, dark place when not in use.

BURDOCK ROOT ECZEMA COMPRESS

1 cup (240 ml) water
2 teaspoons (10 ml) dried burdock root

Burdock root is a time-honored herbal remedy for the treatment of eczema, an irritating condition characterized by itchy, red patches on the skin and scalp. Many skin care products in the natural food aisle make use of burdock root's benefit, but it is just as easy to make your own poultice. Bring the water to a gentle boil. Steep the burdock root in the water for 10 minutes. Strain, then let cool to room temperature. Soak a clean washcloth in the infusion and apply directly to affected areas. Do not apply to open wounds. Let dry and repeat as necessary.

SLIPPERY ELM SKIN PASTE

1 to 2 tablespoons (15 to 30 ml) slippery elm powder
Water, to make a paste

According to natural medicine experts, Native American healers relied on the dried inner bark of the slippery elm to treat a variety of skin conditions. Mix the slippery elm powder with water until a thick paste forms. This paste is loaded with emollients that may provide relief to itchy and inflamed skin. Apply a coat of the paste to the affected skin and leave in place until it is dry. Rinse gently with tepid water and pat dry with a clean towel. Do not use if skin is ruptured.

Slippery Elm

Noticing its use by Native Americans, American colonists adopted slippery elm for their own medicinal purposes. For centuries, slippery elm was one of the most popular North American remedies for just about anything that needed soothing. Around the time of the Civil War, it was even used to treat venereal diseases, as well as hemorrhoids. More recent research indicates that slippery elm may soothe irritations of the mouth and could help to improve bowel habits in people suffering from constipation.

Unlike many herbal preparations that are drawn from the leaves or root of a plant, slippery elm powder is derived from the slippery elm tree's inner bark. It is rich in a type of soluble fiber that swells and becomes gelatinous when mixed with water, so slippery elm can be consumed as a tea, made into a thick paste, or even formed into a lozenge. It is considered by herbal experts to be an effective home remedy for treating sore throats, coughs, and minor skin irritations.

MAKING IT WORK FOR YOU

Because the slippery elm is a giant tree that reaches heights of sixty feet (18 m), you are better off buying some powder prepared from the bark. It is commonly available in most health-food stores. The pale gray powder has a relatively mild aroma reminiscent of maple.

DRY SKIN CLEANSER

¼ cup (60 ml) aloe vera gel

1 teaspoon (5 ml) almond oil

1 teaspoon (5 ml) glycerin

½ teaspoon (3 ml) grapefruit seed extract

8 drops sandalwood essential oil

4 drops rosemary essential oil

If you have dry skin or psoriasis, a genetic skin condition that most commonly presents itself in the form of itchy, red patches topped with silver scales, you may need to avoid most commercial soaps, which tend to be overly drying and irritating to sensitive skin. This herbal skin cleanser is gentle and designed to fight inflammation. Combine the aloe vera gel, almond oil, glycerin, grapefruit seed extract, and essential oils in a small jar or bottle and shake well before using. Apply with cotton balls to the affected skin, then rinse gently with tepid water. Pat the area dry with a clean towel.

Herb Fact

Almond oil is also used to condition wood. Musicians often apply almond oil to instruments such as the clarinet and oboe to keep the wood from drying out.

RASH-SOOTHING RESCUE COMPOUND

2 tablespoons (30 ml) colloidal oatmeal

1-2 drops olive oil

2 tablespoons (30 ml) honey

This simple formula calls upon the rash-soothing reputation of oats. Oats' healing reputation is so convincing that they are found in many commercial products, from diaper cream ointments to facial masks. While this particular remedy is not intended for the diaper region, the combination of oats and honey should work wonders on other areas of the body that are feeling weathered and inflamed. Use colloidal oatmeal because it has already been ground into a very fine powder (the thicker stuff that you cook with works, too, but poses a risk of clogging your drain). Place the oatmeal in a small bowl. Rub a few drops of olive oil in the bottom of your measuring spoon and measure the honey (the oil will help the honey pour from the spoon without sticking). Stir the honey and oatmeal until combined (mixture will be thick). Spread paste onto the affected area and let sit for 20 to 30 minutes. Rinse off with lukewarm water, then pat area dry with a clean towel.

TREE-TEA-OIL-LAVENDER ANTIFUNGAL FOOT SOAK

2 tablespoons (30 ml) almond oil

1 teaspoon (5 ml) tea-tree essential oil

1 teaspoon (5 ml) lavender essential oil

Foot fungus, commonly referred to as athlete's foot, can be easily spread, and if left unchecked, it can eventually infect your toenails, causing discoloration, and in extreme cases, crumbling. Herbal experts suggest incorporating the power of tea-tree oil and lavender into your regular foot care routine to help prevent athlete's foot. Combine the almond, tea-tree, and lavender oils in a small glass jar or bottle and shake well to distribute. Apply a small amount nightly to clean, dry feet, massaging with light strokes until oil is absorbed. Keep the container sealed and store in a cool, dark place when not in use.

Herb Fact

Researchers have found that lavender essential oil shows measurable antifungal activity. It destroyed a variety of fungal cells, including those found in ringworm, athlete's foot, and candida.

INVIGORATING FOOT MASSAGE OIL

2 teaspoons (10 ml) almond or light olive oil

½ teaspoon (3 ml) aloe vera gel

½ teaspoon (3 ml) wheat germ oil

10 drops eucalyptus essential oil

10 drops peppermint essential oil

It is hard to say whether your feet will feel better after this treatment because of the herbs or because you massaged them. Regardless, the combination of peppermint and eucalyptus oils imparts a refreshing scent and light, cooling tingle that will linger after giving your feet the care they deserve. Combine the almond or olive oil, aloe vera gel, wheat germ oil, and essential oils in a small glass bowl. Stir with your finger until well combined, then immediately massage your feet with the formula.

Minor First Aid Treatments

LONG BEFORE CLARA BARTON ORGANIZED THE AMERICAN RED CROSS IN 1881 AND FORMALIZED THE IDEA OF "FIRST AID," people turned to herbs as an accessible means to heal minor injuries. In fact, throughout history, herbs have been on the front lines in emergency treatment. Among other uses, they have been employed to stop bleeding, reduce inflammation, combat pain, soothe burns, and promote wound healing. The efficacy of herbal first aid has been widely acknowledged from ancient times forward. In Homer's *Iliad*, Idomeneus exclaims, "A physician is worth more than several other men put together, for he can cut out arrows and spread healing herbs."

Herbal first aid treatments have been employed in many cultures. Around 300 BCE, the famous practitioner of Ayurvedic medicine, Charaka, wrote an extensive treatise on medicine that included numerous herbal preparations for first aid, including treatments for asthma and vomiting. During the medieval era, the German abbess and botanist Hildegard von Bingen prepared two volumes of botanical and medical information, in which hundreds of herbal remedies are noted, including tansy for an upset stomach. In North America, the Plains Indians used purple coneflower to treat bee stings. In colonial America, wounds were dressed with the leaves of lamb's ears when bandages were not available. Herbal first aid was administered via poultices, liniments, and soaks, among other methods.

Herbal first aid treatments, some remarkably unchanged over time, have been continuously employed into modern times. In this section, we will review some of the most efficacious options for treating minor problems. Do note, however, that these remedies do not substitute for professional care; any injury or symptom that does not clear up swiftly should be seen by a medical professional. And the following problems require medical care in every case: any burn that is extremely tender, painful, swollen, or blistered, or accompanied by fever; any burn that has pus, yellowish drainage, or yellowish crust; and any instance in which the area around the burn looks red or feels hot. With bee or insect stings, allergies can be deadly. Seek emergency medical care for anyone experiencing swelling in the mouth or throat, rash all over the body, or difficulty breathing or speaking. If a cut is large (more than ½ inch [1 cm] long) or deep into the yellow, fatty layer of your skin, seek medical care to determine if stitches and/or antibiotics are necessary.

PARSLEY ICE FOR BRUISES

½ cup (30 g) fresh parsley
¼ cup (60 ml) water

According to herbal folklore, parsley has long been effective at easing the inflammation and fading the color of bruises. Place the parsley and water in a blender and combine until mixture is slushy. Transfer the mixture to an ice-cube tray and freeze until ice cubes form. To use, wrap an ice cube in a piece of gauze or paper towel and place it directly on the bruised area for 15 to 20 minutes. (Do not place ice directly on the skin.)

Herb Fact

Parsley was considered bad luck in ancient Greece. Soldiers would go out of their way to avoid contact with parsley before battle because they believed it was a sign of impending death.

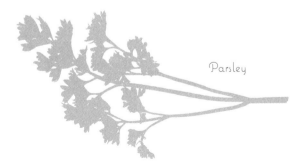

Parsley

CALENDULA BRUISE POULTICE

1 to 2 tablespoons (15 to 30 ml) dried calendula
1 to 2 tablespoons (15 to 30 ml) water

Bruises occur when blood vessels break beneath the surface of your skin and leak small amounts of blood, causing pain, discoloration, and sometimes swelling. Of course, most bruises heal on their own in a couple of weeks, but you may be able to shorten that time frame and ease some of the pain in the process by applying this easy-to-prepare poultice as soon as possible. Soak the dried calendula in an equal amount of water for a few minutes until the flowers rehydrate. Place the calendula directly on the bruise and secure in place with an adhesive bandage (or gauze and tape, if the area is larger). Keep the poultice in place for 3 to 4 hours. If you have fresh calendula available in your garden (it is more commonly known as pot marigold), simply crush some petals and apply directly to the bruised area. Rarely, calendula can cause a rash; if you have sensitive skin, test a small patch before applying the poultice.

Calendula

Calendula

A BRIEF HISTORY

A member of the daisy family, calendula was given its name by the ancient Romans, who took note that the flower was in bloom on the first day of every month. They saw its nearly constant blooming to be a sign of joy and grew it in their gardens to spread happiness. Calendula came by its common name, pot marigold, because it was so popular as a culinary herb that it was added to nearly every pot.

Many different herbal traditions have employed calendula for a wide variety of ailments, from conjunctivitis to athlete's foot. One twelfth-century physician believed just looking at it could improve the eyesight! Today, research shows that calendula's constituents have antibacterial, anti-inflammatory, and antiparasitic properties. Calendula can be used externally to soothe minor cuts and scrapes, as well as sunburns and rashes. It should be avoided during pregnancy and lactation.

MAKING IT WORK FOR YOU

Do not confuse calendula (*Calendula officinalis*) with the more commmon garden marigold (*Tagetes*). An easy-to-grow perennial, calendula will grow even more rapidly if you remove its flowers regularly. Dry the entire head if you like, or look for calendula as a tea or tincture in your local health-food store.

COMFREY ICE PACK

1 cup (240 ml) water
2 teaspoons (10 ml) dried comfrey

Comfrey is a hardy perennial that's favored by herbal experts for its versatility in healing bites, burns, rashes, stings, and cuts, as well as the occasional muscle sprain. When pounded into a paste, comfrey hardens like a plaster, and according to history experts, ancient Greeks and Romans used it on battlefields to help set broken bones. Comfrey contains high levels of a chemical that can cause liver damage, so experts advise that it is for external use only. Bring water to a gentle boil. Steep the comfrey in the water for 10 minutes. Strain, then let cool to room temperature, keeping it covered to retain the volatile oils. Transfer liquid to an ice-cube tray and freeze until ice cubes form. To use, wrap an ice cube in a piece of gauze or paper towel and place it directly on the bruised area for 15 to 20 minutes. (Do not place ice directly on the skin.)

Comfrey

SUPERB SUNBURN SPRAY

½ cup (120 ml) aloe vera juice

1 tablespoon (15 ml) vinegar

1 teaspoon (5 ml) vitamin E oil

½ teaspoon (3 ml) lavender essential oil

Herbal experts credit both lavender essential oil and aloe vera as having the ability to reduce inflammation. So this powerful duo together in a sunburn spray makes a classic combination. Do not confuse aloe vera juice with the gel, which will make the spray too thick; both are usually available in health-food stores. Combine the aloe vera juice, vinegar, vitamin E, and lavender essential oil in a small spray bottle. Shake before each use and spray generously onto the affected area. Store the spray in the refrigerator in between uses to keep the ingredients fresh and to improve the cooling effect.

Herb Fact

Legends tell that Alexander the Great sent his army to seize an island known for growing aloe vera plants so that his soldiers could readily enjoy the benefits of the plant's amazing wound-healing properties.

Aloe Vera

The use of aloe as a healing plant goes back thousands of years. Aloe vera is thought to have originated in Africa; it soon spread to Europe and Asia, and is now cultivated around the world. Aloe is a succulent plant, which means it has adapted to living under hot, arid conditions by storing water in its leaves; however, in the case of the aloe plant, the "water" is actually a gel with amazing antibacterial and antifungal properties that can provide quick pain relief and help speed healing.

In ancient Egypt, aloe vera was known as "plant of immortality"; no fewer than a dozen formulas listed in the Ebers Papyrus include aloe vera. The first-century physician Dioscorides described it as a good topical treatment for bruises, hemorrhoids, and dry skin, among other conditions. By the ninth century, the great Arab, scientist, philosopher, and physician al-Kindi wrote in his *Medical Formulary* that aloe vera was useful in the treatment of boils and abscesses. In the sixteenth century, English herbalist John Gerard recommended aloe vera to clean wounds. Recent research confirms that aloe vera can indeed be very helpful in the treatment of burns, and may have other significant healing properties as well.

Aloe is easy to use for a variety of topical skin injuries, from sunburns to insect bites, as well as dry, itchy skin. Simply break off a piece of the leaf and scrape out the healing gel inside. Keep in mind that aloe is not appropriate for internal use as it can cause painful cramps; do not ingest it.

MAKING IT WORK FOR YOU

A semitropical plant, aloe vera prefers warm, sunny conditions. It won't be happy outdoors if the temperature dips below 40°F (4°C), so in cooler climates it is mostly cultivated as a houseplant. It is extremely easy to grow on a sunny windowsill. Do not overwater, as aloe is a succulent—experts recommend a thorough soaking, then waiting until the soil has fully dried before watering again. In northern climates, a potted aloe vera may be taken outdoors during the summer, but be sure to bring it indoors well before frost. When it is time to bring your plant back inside for the winter, you may be rewarded with dozens of little offsets that you can dig up to share with friends.

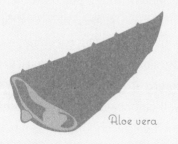

Aloe vera

ALOE BURN RELIEVER

Potted aloe plant

Keeping a potted aloe plant on your kitchen windowsill means that you can offer immediate relief for mild burns. Aloe is especially easy to grow and has been used for centuries to promote healthy skin. It is loaded with vitamins C and E and helps reduce swelling while dilating capillaries, making it easier for the skin to heal itself. Simply break off a piece of the aloe plant's spiky leaf and squeeze the gel inside directly onto the affected area.

CUCUMBER SUNBURN LOTION

1 cucumber
2 tablespoons (30 ml) glycerin
2 tablespoons (30 ml) rose water

Cucumbers may be 96 percent water, but the other 4 percent contains just the right mix of cooling, skin-soothing nutrients for treating sunburn. To collect the juices, grate the cucumber over a large bowl then squeeze even more liquid from the grated cucumber. Mix the cucumber juice with the glycerin and rose water in a small jar. Shake until ingredients are well combined. Refrigerate until ready to use. Apply a thin coat to affected area and repeat as necessary.

COMFREY POISON IVY COMPRESS

1 cup (240 ml) water
2 teaspoons (10 ml) dried comfrey

Poison ivy is a plant that contains urushiol, one of the most misery-inducing allergenic oils on the planet. If you're exposed, your skin will soon develop the telltale itchy and painful rash. For relief, turn to the inflammation-fighting power of comfrey. If you have access to the fresh plant, squeeze out some comfrey juice from the stems of the plant and rub it on the rash. If the dried herb is your only option, try this herbal compress remedy. Bring water to a gentle boil. Steep the comfrey in the water for 10 minutes. Strain, then let cool to room temperature, keeping it covered to retain the volatile oils. Soak a clean cloth in the infusion and apply directly to affected areas. Let dry and repeat as necessary. (Note that comfrey is not to be taken internally; it is for topical use only. Do not apply to broken skin.)

Herb Fact

The word "comfrey" is derived from the Latin *conferta*, which means "grow together." Comfrey was employed by the ancient Greeks and Romans to close wound and treat broken bones.

ECHINACEA BEE STING REMEDY

1 teaspoon (5 ml) green clay powder
1 teaspoon (5 ml) distilled water
1 teaspoon (5 ml) echinacea tincture

Herbal experts credit a dab of clay on a bee sting for providing a quick, natural means to instant, cooling relief. As the clay dries, it causes the skin to shrink temporarily, helping to draw out the stinger and subdue the accompanying toxins. A bit of echinacea tincture added to the mix may prompt faster healing. Combine the green clay powder, water, and echinacea tincture in a small bowl and stir with your finger until thoroughly mixed. Apply to a fresh insect bite or sting. Rinse with cool water when the clay is dry and the itching or stinging has subsided.

INSECT BITE OIL

1 tablespoon (15 ml) vegetable oil
1 teaspoon (5 ml) lavender essential oil

For minor bug bites, and the irritating itch that accompanies them, consider carrying this lavender-based insect bite oil with you the next time you venture into the great outdoors. This folkloric formula calls for a 1 to 3 ratio of lavender essential oil to plain vegetable oil. Combine the vegetable and lavender oils in a small glass jar and shake well to distribute. Dab a small amount directly on fresh bug bites. Keep oil sealed and store in a cool, dark place when not in use.

QUICK CHAMOMILE POULTICE
FOR MINOR CUTS AND SCRAPES

1 chamomile tea bag
1 to 2 tablespoons (15 to 30 ml) warm water

In Europe, chamomile is considered a cure-all herb; in Germany, it is commonly referred to as *alles zutraut*, which translates to "capable of anything." Even if you prefer brewing your own loose tea, keeping a box of chamomile tea bags on hand will provide ready access to this easy go-to poultice for minor cuts and scrapes that may help ease inflammation and fight bacteria. Soak tea bag in water for a minute or so to activate the tea. Place over a cut or scrape, which has been thoroughly cleaned with soap and water, then press gently. Secure tea bag in place with gauze and let sit for 20 to 30 minutes. Alternately, if you have some chamomile tea already made, simply soak gauze pads in the liquid and proceed with the rest of the instructions.

ROSEMARY MUSCLE RUB

¼ cup (60 ml) almond oil
15 drops rosemary essential oil
10 drops juniper essential oil
10 drops wintergreen essential oil

You can call upon the restorative power of herbs to help work out the occasional soreness related to muscle cramps. This particular combination draws on rosemary and mentholated herbs, with scents you will recognize from over-the-counter muscle rubs, to help loosen things up. Combine the almond, rosemary, juniper, and wintergreen oils in a small glass jar and shake well to distribute. Gently rub oil onto affected areas. Keep oil sealed and store in a cool, dark place when not in use.

Herb Fact

Rosemary is believed to have been a favorite scent of Napoleon Bonaparte, whose eau de cologne featured this herb.

SPLINTER REMEDY

1 teaspoon (5 ml) baking soda
1 to 2 drops lavender essential oil
Water, to make a paste

Finding a splinter in the tender skin of your finger or foot is definitely unpleasant, but fortunately most splinters eventually come out on their own. However, if you have a particularly stubborn splinter to deal with, experts advise first washing the affected area with soap and water, and then trying this homemade poultice to make the extraction easier. Mix a teaspoon of baking soda and a few drops of lavender essential oil with enough water to make a thick paste. Spread the paste gently over the splinter and top with a small piece of gauze secured with first aid tape. Let the poultice set for 1 to 2 hours, then remove the bandage and rinse the paste off. If the splinter hasn't already come out on its own, use tweezers to grab the splinter and back it out of the skin. Follow up with a dab of antiseptic ointment and seek further care if signs of infection develop.

PART 2

Your Herbal Home

Herbs Indoors and Out

Oregano

IF ASKED TO SUGGEST PRACTICAL WAYS TO USE HERBS, most people probably would start with culinary uses, then move on to healing—but the power of herbs extends beyond the kitchen and medicine cabinet to the rest of the home and garden! In the pages that follow, you will find a wealth of household solutions based on herbs. Household herbal traditions have every bit as long and effective a history as culinary and medical uses. Indeed, whether it's placing rosemary-filled sachets in your closets to discourage moths or stuffing a lemon rind into the garbage disposal to fill your kitchen with its fresh, clean scent, you may already be using herbs to make your home more pleasant.

It's no accident that many commercial home products include herbs. For example, a quick perusal of popular all-purpose cleansers at the grocery store yields ingredients such as lavender, citrus oils, and tea-tree oil. All of these herbs have powerful antimicrobial, antifungal, and antibacterial properties. And they can make a product appear more "natural" to consumers, too, highlighting a common desire for a less toxic approach to cleaning.

As the formulas in the following pages demonstrate, all you need are some very basic ingredients—versatile products like vinegar, castile soap, baking soda, and borax, along with some spray bottles and lidded containers—to transform your herb supplies into a fully loaded cleaning arsenal suitable for any room in the house. In minutes you can whip up a fresh batch of laundry soap or glass cleaner that will cost far less than the commercial products would, and you'll save valuable storage space along the way because many of these formulas are multipurpose and can tackle several tasks at once.

Laundry Room and Closet Invigorators

IF YOU TAKE A STROLL DOWN THE DETERGENT AISLE OF ANY SUPERMARKET, you will see a number of herb-scented products. Using herbs to lend pleasing aromas to detergent goes way back to the beginnings of soap. Arab traders were responsible for introducing bar soap to Europe around the seventh century. Those early soaps were typically made from animal fats or olive oil mixed with wood ash; plant material was added to improve the scent. In Europe, these soaps were used mostly for laundry—it was not until the Renaissance that people began using soap for personal cleansing.

Beyond adding a nice fragrance, there's a practical reason why manufacturers of detergent in any era would include herbal additives: herbs can boost cleaning power, specifically through their essential oils.

The good news for you is that you do not have to abandon your favorite laundry products to reap the rewards of a fresh, herbal clean; in this section you will find some formulas that offer ways of adding the power of herbs to existing products. Additionally, there are homemade options that offer some less expensive, natural alternatives for your laundry routine.

Of course, herbs can help outside the laundry room, too. Herbs have long been employed to keep closets and cupboards fresh, nicely scented, and free of pests. In this section, you'll also discover herbal solutions for keeping clothing and linens pristine.

DUST MITE DETERRENT

Laundry soap of your choice, enough for one load
25 drops or 1 tablespoon (15 ml) eucalyptus essential oil,
    depending on your washing machine

If you find that you wake with allergy symptoms in the morning—itchy, puffy eyes and a stuffy nose—you might be suffering from the all-too-common dust mite allergy. Dust mites are microscopic bugs that feed off dead skin cells, so they tend to congregate in bedding. For those with allergies, the mites aren't the real problem; the problem is the protein in the waste they leave behind. Research has shown that eucalyptus essential oil, used regularly in the laundry, can help keep dust mites at bay. If you have a top-loading machine, start your wash as usual, using the laundry soap of your choice. Once the washer is filled, open the top and add 25 drops of eucalyptus essential oil, then let the machine finish the load as usual. If you have a front-loading machine, add 1 tablespoon (15 ml) of eucalyptus oil to an entire bottle of laundry soap to achieve the same effect. Just make sure to shake well to distribute the oil.

Eucalyptus

A BRIEF HISTORY

Among the hundreds of species of eucalyptus, all of which origi-nated in Australia, the type that is most often used medicinally is called blue gum or Australian fever tree. Like other members of the myrtle family, eucalyptus has leaves that produce an abundance of volatile oil, which is extremely flammable. In fact, the vaporized oil of the eucalyptus plant is credited with lending the Australian landscape its distinct blue haze on warm days.

The aboriginal people of Australia used eucalyptus for healing wounds; there is evidence that other ancient cultures, including those of Egypt and India, also used eucalyptus medicinally. Euca-lyptus was introduced to the West via the diaries of Abel Tasman, who noted while on a voyage of discovery in December 1642 the unusual trees with gum leaking from them. By the nineteenth cen-tury, hospitals in England used eucalyptus oil to clean tubes; since then, laboratory studies have shown that the oil does indeed pos-sess antibacterial properties. Today, however, the most common medicinal use for eucalyptus is in treating coughs and congestion associated with the common cold. Its pungent aroma and expec-torant action make it especially useful as an inhalant. Outside the medicine cabinet, eucalyptus is commonly added to detergents, soaps, and perfumes for its fresh scent.

Eucalyptus trees are now grown on every continent in semitropical to semiarid climates. For most of the formulas in this book, you will need only the basic essential oil product, which can be found in your local health-food store. If you're intrigued by the idea of bringing the scent of fresh eucalyptus into your house, your best bet (unless you live in a warm climate) will be to buy fresh eucalyptus branches instead of trying to grow it yourself, as most eucalyptus species do not tolerate frost well. Shop for fresh branches at your local farmers' market, online, or at your local florist.

Eucalyptus

TEA-TREE OIL LAUNDRY SOAP

½ gallon (2 l) water

½ bar Fels-Naptha laundry soap, grated

1 cup (220 g) washing soda

1 cup (220 g) borax

1½ gallons (6 l) warm water

15 drops tea-tree oil

If you have a large household and find yourself doing several loads of laundry every day, this formula could save you a lot of money over the course of the year. You will need a large lidded bucket for making and storing the formula (or recycle some empty laundry detergent bottles for storage). Warm ¼ gallon (1 l) water in a large saucepan over medium heat. Add the grated soap and stir until dissolved (this may take several minutes). Remove from heat and add the other ¼ gallon (1 l) water, the washing soda, and the borax. Mix thoroughly. Pour the mixture into a large bucket and add the remaining 1½ gallons (6 l) warm water. Stir until ingredients are thoroughly combined, then add the tea-tree oil. Place the lid on the bucket and let detergent sit overnight before using or transferring to other containers. Always stir before using and store with the lid on. You will only need to use ¼ to ⅓ cup (60 to 80 ml) per load. The batch should last for about one hundred wash cycles.

GENTLE SOAPWORT SOAP

4 cups (950 ml) distilled or filtered water

2 cups (43 g) chopped fresh or 1 cup (43 g) dried soapwort

¼ cup dried (12 g) lavender, optional

Soapwort is an herb your grandmother may have used to launder her favorite delicate linens, and it may be making a comeback as more and more people turn to natural cleaning methods around the home. It contains saponins, which when mixed with water, create a light, foamy lather. Soapwort is an easy-to-grow perennial ground cover, so you could easily have your own supply from your garden. Bring the water to a gentle boil. Add the soapwort and lavender, if using. Steep the herbs, covered, for 15 minutes. Allow to cool to room temperature, then strain the mixture through a small sieve lined with a coffee filter or cheesecloth. Swish the water to create gentle, sudsy foam and use as you would any soap for delicate, washable fabrics.

LOVELY LEMON LAUNDRY SOAP

1 cup (240 ml) liquid castile soap
1/4 cup (60 ml) aloe vera juice
1/4 cup (60 ml) white vinegar
1/2 cup (475 ml) water
10 to 15 drops lemon essential oil

There's something truly satisfying about making a fresh batch of a homemade cleaning supply, and this formula will get you through about eight average loads of laundry. If you don't have any aloe vera juice handy, double the amount of vinegar. Combine the soap, aloe vera juice, vinegar, water, and essential oil in a container with a lid. Shake gently a few times to mix ingredients and use as you would commercial laundry soap (about 1/4 cup [60 ml] per load).

Herb Fact

The origins of the lemon tree remain unknown, though many scientists believe it originated in Southeast Asia. Now it is grown all over the world.

LAVENDER LAUNDRY SOFTENER

3 cups (700 ml) white vinegar

3 cups (700 ml) distilled water

1 teaspoon (5 ml) lavender essential oil

Vinegar has a wonderful reputation as a natural fabric softener. The mild acidic properties of vinegar do a great job at breaking down soap proteins to make your wash truly clean. But some people resist putting vinegar to such good use because they find its sour scent unpleasant. If you've been hesitant to give vinegar a try in the laundry room, consider adding a little lavender essential oil to make things more sweetly aromatic. Combine the vinegar, water, and lavender essential oil in a large plastic jar with a lid. Shake vigorously to combine ingredients. Use approximately 1 cup (240 ml) per load, added during the rinse cycle.

Lavender

A BRIEF HISTORY

The fresh, clean scent of lavender probably explains how this popular Mediterranean herb got its name from the Latin verb *lavare*, meaning "to wash." There are more than twenty-five species of the plant to choose from, of which English lavender is generally considered the most fragrant. The volatile oil found in its blossoms contains more than a hundred chemical compounds, and in a good year, one acre (4,047 sq m) of this particular plant will produce fifteen to twenty pounds (7 to 9 kg) of highly prized essential oil.

As with many herbs that have ancient roots, the exact origin of lavender remains a mystery, though it is believed to have first been cultivated in the Middle East. It spread rapidly throughout the Mediterranean, where it was prized for its scent and medicinal qualities. Dioscorides wrote of it in the first century, noting its laxative action, while Pliny the Elder recommended it for bereavement. It was a popular addition to Roman baths. Hildegard von Bingen attributed many virtues to lavender, including the treatment of lice, and it has remained well regarded among herbalists to the present day.

Traditionally, dried lavender blossoms have been used in sachets to protect linens from moths and to bring a pleasing scent to sickrooms. During the seventeenth-century Great Plague, glove makers believed lavender was a good way to ward off disease and relied on its oil to scent their leather. They may have had the right idea since it is now known that fleas transmit the plague, and lavender is an effective insect repellent. Many aromatherapists also believe lavender can impart a serious benefit as a stress reliever, so it is frequently added to massage oils and bath-related remedies. Studies reveal that lavender has antibacterial properties; other studies indicate that lavender may indeed relieve anxiety.

MAKING IT WORK FOR YOU

If you want to grow your own lavender, head to a reliable plant nursery to find your best options. Lavender is rarely grown from seed; it is an ideal plant for container gardening. It is a sun-loving perennial. To dry lavender for later use, clip the stems, just before the flowers bloom, and then hang them in bunches. Allow to dry in a shaded, airy place with high temperatures (attic rafters are ideal for this).

Lavender

NATURAL DRYER SHEET

10 to 15 drops lavender, lemon, or bergamot essential oil

Washcloth

While this natural dryer sheet won't reduce static cling like the commercial products, you will notice your clothes smelling particularly fresh and lovely after a cycle in the dryer. Dampen a washcloth and wring it out. Sprinkle with 10 to 15 drops of your favorite essential oil and toss in the dryer with clean, wet laundry. Dry as usual.

FRENCH IRONING WATER

4 cups (950 ml) distilled or purified water

1/8 teaspoon (1 ml) lavender essential oil

The French are renowned for their love of lavender—in the South of France, vast fields of lavender give Provence some of its most beautiful vistas. Lavender lovers look for every opportunity to slip the seductive, fresh scent into their daily routine. Consider this easy method of adding a whiff of lavender into your next load of ironing. Use purified or distilled water for best results. Combine water and essential oil in a large spray bottle and shake vigorously before using. Spritz dry, clean clothes, and then iron as usual.

WINTER STORAGE MOTH-REPELLING SACHETS

1 cup (34 g) dried mint
1 cup (53 g) dried rosemary

As summer draws to a close, you might be faced with more fresh herbs than you can handle. But with winter just around the corner, you will have plenty of time to dry those herbs and put together some easy sachets that will help keep moths away from your stored clothing and linens. Harvest and dry your herbs according to the directions on page 22. Combine equal amounts of mint and rosemary in a large bowl and break the herbs into smaller pieces, if necessary. Take care not to let them crumble. Lay a clean linen handkerchief in front of you (a piece of cheesecloth of about the same size will also do nicely) and place about ½ cup of the mixture in the center. Gather the corners together, tucking the herbs tightly in the center; secure the neck of the pouch with a rubber band. Cover the rubber band with a decorative ribbon, if desired, and distribute among the clean clothes and linens that you are packing away for the season.

Rosemary

SEW-EASY ROSE SACHETS

Linen handkerchief

Sewing needle

24 inches (60 cm) thread

1 decorative button

2 handfuls rose petals

3 to 5 drops rose essential oil

These quick sachets are perfect for gift giving. Lay the handkerchief on a flat surface with the pattern side up. Fold 3 corners toward the square's center so that they overlap slightly, forming a pouch or envelope. Hand-stitch the edges together, then sew a seam along the sides of the envelope. Turn the sachet inside out, press, and sew a decorative button atop the flap. Fill the pouch with dried rose petals and a few drops of rose essential oil. Secure the flap by carefully adding some hidden stitches along the underside, about 1/4 inch (6 mm) inside the outer edge. Tuck into lingerie drawers, bathroom cabinets, clothes closets, or wherever you would like to enjoy the scent of rose.

Herb Fact

Fossil evidence suggests that roses may date back 35 million years. They were likely first cultivated in China some 5,000 years ago.

SIMPLE LINEN CLOSET-FRESHENING POUCHES

Premade organza or muslin drawstring bags
Lavender buds or flowers

Linens are often stored in a closed closet for a long time, and they can quickly lose that just-washed freshness. To prevent your linens from getting a musty or stale odor, make a few of these easy, no-sew, herbal pouches. Little muslin or organza bags are available at many crafts stores. If you have grown and dried your own lavender, simply hold the stems in one hand and strip the buds with the other. Don't worry if you haven't dried your own lavender—many herbal-products stores, farmer's market stands, and online resources sell lavender in bulk. Scoop several spoonfuls of lavender into each bag, filling fully but not till bursting. Tie off with the drawstrings. These little bags are great for tucking in among your linens, or anywhere else you would enjoy the scent of lavender. When the scent fades, you can renew with more buds or a drop or two of lavender essential oil.

Herb Fact

By the seventeenth century, lavender was so well known that the English herbalist Culpeper gave no details in his herbal, saying instead, "This is so well known, being an Inhabitant in almost every Garden, that it needeth no Description."

Kitchen Helpers

IT'S NO SURPRISE TO FIND HERBS BEING PUT TO GOOD USE IN THE KITCHEN when dinner is under way. Having read this far, you probably also know that many herbs also contain antibacterial properties. That makes them ideal ingredients in a variety of homemade cleaning products.

The use of herbs as disinfectants has examples throughout history. An herbal concoction known as "Four Thieves Vinegar" that contained rue, rosemary, and lavender, among other herbs, dates back to the Middle Ages, when it was used to disinfect surfaces to protect against the plague. "Strewing herbs," including hyssop and meadowsweet, were scattered over floors in churches, temples, and monasteries, as well as hospitals and jails, not only to sweeten the air, but because they were believed to have antiseptic properties.

Today, studies show that many of the herbs used for these purposes in history do exhibit antibacterial effects. Continuing research is focusing on a wide variety of herbs and their essential oils, including basil, caraway, cinnamon, eucalyptus, nutmeg, oregano, sage, tea tree, thyme, and many others, which may be useful as antibacterials. All the more reason to incorporate herbs into your kitchen-cleaning routine!

As powerful chemicals have been shown to cause harm to both humans and the environment, more and more people have grown concerned about the possible toxicity of commercial cleaning products. This has led many to discover the reassuringly nontoxic and effective cleansing power of herbal formulas. Why not try out a few of these homemade cleaning options—they'll make tidying up the kitchen a more pleasant prospect!

NATURAL FLOOR WASH

2 gallons (8 l) warm water
¼ cup (60 ml) white vinegar
10 drops lemon or pine essential oil

Contrary to conventional wisdom, using soap to clean a floor can lead to a buildup of soapy residue that actually traps more dirt over time. Many types of flooring are best cleaned with plain old water mixed with a splash of vinegar. However, if you'd like to enjoy a fresh, clean fragrance while you clean, consider giving this formula a try. Combine the water, vinegar, and essential oil of your choice in a large bucket, then clean floors as usual.

Herb Fact

Pine trees are native to the Northern Hemisphere. There are more than a hundred species of pine, but most pine essential oil is distilled from the needles, twigs, and cones of the Scotch pine.

EUCALYPTUS-MINT LIQUID SOAP

½ cup (17 g) dried or 1 cup (12 g) fresh peppermint

6 cups (1.5 l) water

5 cups (550 g) castile soap, grated

½ cup (110 g) baking soda

1 teaspoon (5 ml) borax, optional

1 teaspoon (5 ml) eucalyptus essential oil

Liquid soaps are extremely popular and easy to use, but they're relatively expensive when you consider how much can be saved by making your own formula. Bundle the peppermint into a piece of cheesecloth and bring the water to a gentle boil in a large stainless steel saucepan. Turn the heat to low, place the cheesecloth in the pot, and cover. Let simmer for 15 minutes. Remove the peppermint and add the grated soap to the liquid. Let simmer another 15 minutes on low heat, occasionally giving the mixture a gentle stir until soap has melted. Remove from heat. Stir in the baking soda, borax, if using, and eucalyptus oil, then let cool to room temperature. Store in a labeled plastic jug or squirt bottle and shake gently before using.

JUST-IN-THYME DISINFECTANT CLEANSER

2½ cups (600 ml) water
1 handful fresh or dried thyme
1 cup (240 ml) white vinegar
¼ teaspoon (1.5 ml) liquid castile soap

Keeping a natural disinfectant handy in the kitchen is crucial because overgrowth of some kinds of bacteria can lead to a variety of food-borne illnesses. And if you abhor the idea of using harsh chemicals around your food, then this gentle yet effective formula might just be the cleanser for you. Bring the water to a gentle boil in a large stainless steel saucepan. Turn the heat to low, place the thyme in the pot, and cover. Let simmer for 1 hour, then let sit until cool. Strain the liquid into a 24-ounce (700-ml) spray bottle, filling it to the top with white vinegar and adding one squirt (about ¼ teaspoon [3 ml]) of liquid castile soap. Use as needed to clean and disinfect a variety of surfaces in the kitchen, including the stove, countertops, and cutting boards.

Thyme

A BRIEF HISTORY

Thyme, a member of the mint family, was commonly used as incense during important ceremonies in ancient Greek temples. The popular herb was also associated with courage and bravery through the Middle Ages, during which it was often tied to symbolic scarves exchanged between maidens and knights.

Thyme's essential oils contain large amounts of thymol, a strong antibacterial agent. Used in a mouthwash, it can help treat inflammation and infection. Thyme is also put to good use in natural cough drops because it can help ease the spasms associated with coughing fits, as well as loosen congestion. Around the house, thyme's strong antibacterial properties make it a valuable ingredient in many natural-cleaning formulas.

MAKING IT WORK FOR YOU

Thyme can be used fresh or dried for many of the formulas in this book, but if you want to grow your own, there are a number of varieties, with the most popular being common or garden thyme. It is a short perennial with stiff woody stems and small gray-green leaves. For best results, plant thyme in full sun in loose, well-drained soil. Each spring, examine your plant carefully and prune damaged stems to ensure new growth. In summer, thyme's fragrant, lilac-pink flowers will appear in clusters and can attract many bees.

EUCALYPTUS ALL-PURPOSE KITCHEN SPRAY

2 tablespoons (30 ml) white vinegar

1 tablespoon (15 ml) borax

2 cups (475 ml) hot distilled water

¼ cup (60 ml) liquid castile soap

10 to 15 drops eucalyptus essential oil

It is best to use distilled water with this formula because the minerals naturally present in tap water can hamper the product's cleaning ability. Also, make sure to combine ingredients in this formula exactly as directed; if the borax is not dissolved properly, it could clog the bottle nozzle (use a clear bottle, if possible, so you can see what's going on). Combine vinegar and borax in a 16-ounce (475-ml) spray bottle. Fill bottle almost to top with very hot distilled water and shake until borax is dissolved. Add the soap and essential oil, then cap tightly. Shake lightly to distribute the soap throughout the mixture.

LAVENDER SOFT SCRUB

$^{3}/_{4}$ cup (165 g) baking soda

$^{1}/_{4}$ cup (30 g) powdered milk

5 drops lavender essential oil

$^{1}/_{4}$ teaspoon (1.5 ml) liquid castile soap

Water, to make a paste

While being surprisingly gentle, baking soda has a solid reputation for taking on tough stains and spills. Its texture gives baking soda extra cleaning power. Combine the baking soda, powdered milk, and essential oil in a small plastic container with a tight-fitting lid. Shake vigorously to combine ingredients, and then set aside in a cool, dark place until you're ready to use. To make a batch of soft scrub, simply scoop a spoonful (or two) of the mixture into a small bowl. Add a squirt of liquid castile soap and just enough water to make a smooth paste. Use with a damp sponge to gently clean nonporous surfaces, and then rinse thoroughly with fresh water.

Lavender

LEMON-THYME MICROWAVE CLEANER

¼ cup (55 g) baking soda

1 tablespoon (15 ml) white vinegar

3 to 4 drops thyme essential oil

3 to 4 drops lemon essential oil

This hardworking formula is a cinch to put together, and one batch makes plenty to get the inside of your microwave sparkling clean. If you don't have both types of essential oil, just use whatever combination you like best. Combine the baking soda, vinegar, and essential oils in a small glass bowl. Stir gently to make a paste. Apply to the walls and floor of the microwave with a damp, soft cloth or sponge. Rinse well and leave the oven door open for 30 minutes until dry.

BLISSFUL DISHWASHING SOAP

1 cup (240 ml) liquid castile soap

1 cup (240 ml) water

5 drops orange essential oil

3 drops bergamot essential oil

2 drops lavender essential oil

Castile soap takes its name from the region in Spain where the plant-based soap originates, but now it is made around the world under many different brands. And while it is common to find it already scented in many cleaning products, you can save a little money by coming up with your own signature combination. Fill a 16-ounce (475-ml) plastic squirt bottle with castile soap, water, and essential oils. Shake gently to blend. Use as you would commercial dishwashing soap.

Herb Fact

Pure castile soap is made from olive oil, with no animal ingredients.

ALL-NATURAL DISHWASHER SOAP

½ cup (120 ml) liquid castile soap

½ cup (120 ml) water

1 teaspoon (5 ml) fresh lemon juice

3 drops tea-tree oil

¼ cup (60 ml) white vinegar

½ cup (110 g) baking soda for every load

If you use this homemade dishwasher soap as an alternative to a commercial chlorine-based detergent, you will save money and enjoy sparkling clean results. Combine the soap, water, lemon juice, tea-tree oil, and vinegar in a 12-ounce (350-ml) squeeze bottle. Shake gently to distribute ingredients well and store in a cool, dark place. To use, sprinkle a handful of baking soda over dirty dishes. Place 1 tablespoon (15 ml) of the mixture in the soap dispenser; if your dishwasher has another slot for the first part of the wash cycle, add another tablespoon (15 ml) to that compartment as well. Run the dishwasher as usual.

SPONGE CLEANERS

2 to 3 drops citrus-based essential oil, such as orange or lemon

Would it surprise you to learn that your kitchen sponge is quite likely one of the most contaminated objects in your home? Damp sponges provide an ideal breeding ground for bacteria and can be teeming with millions of bacteria after just a few days of use. Even worse is the thought that using a contaminated sponge to "clean" your counters or dishes means you're essentially spreading those germs around even more. To keep your cellulose sponge in tip-top shape, get in the habit of microwaving it on HIGH power for a minute or two every few days, which will effectively kill 99% of the bacteria. When the sponge is cool enough to handle, sprinkle it with a few drops of orange essential oil and squeeze gently to distribute throughout the sponge. Along with a fresh, citrus scent, the oil's demonstrated antibacterial properties will help slow down bacterial growth in between cleanings.

GLASS CLEANER

½ cup (120 ml) dried lavender or thyme
1 cup (240 ml) white vinegar
½ cup (120 ml) water

The power of vinegar is a well-known resource for cleaning glass and
other shiny kitchen surfaces. However, not everyone appreciates vinegar's distinct scent. If you prefer a sweeter smelling clean, similar to
the expensive herbal cleansers you can buy in a store, try this at-home
formula instead. Combine the lavender or thyme and vinegar in a wide-
mouth glass bottle with a tight-fitting lid (a large jelly jar works well).
Store in a cool, dark place for approximately 2 weeks. Shake the jar
gently every day or two so that the contents don't settle. After a couple
of weeks have passed, strain the mixture through a small sieve lined
with a coffee filter or cheesecloth. Transfer the vinegar glass cleaner
to a plastic spray bottle and dilute with ½ cup of water. Shake well and
spray directly onto glass surfaces, then wipe dry with a newspaper for
a streak-free shine.

Thyme

TRASH CAN CURE

2 cups (440 g) baking soda
1 teaspoon (5 ml) lavender essential oil,
    or other essential oil of your choice

Kitchen garbage odors can be especially difficult to control in a smaller household; when trash is slower to accumulate, the offensive elements have more time to grow and multiply in the garbage can, rendering it thoroughly stinky. It's no wonder scented kitchen garbage bags have grown in popularity the last couple of years. However, if you have built up a collection of essential oils, there's no need to resort to expensive bags to keep your trash odors well contained. Simply mix the 2 cups of baking soda and a teaspoon of lavender essential oil (use any kind of oil you like, in fact). Store mixture in a decorative shaker container and sprinkle a few rounds in the bottom of your clean garbage can liner whenever you put a fresh bag in. If necessary, you can always top it off with a few more shakes, especially if you have to dispose of something else potentially smelly before trash collection day.

APPLE PIE POTPOURRI

2 cups (475 ml) water

1 stick cinnamon

6 cloves

3 to 4 pieces dried apple

If you like the smell of freshly baked apple pie but don't want the actual dessert around to tempt you, this simple potpourri is for you. Place the water, cinnamon, cloves, and dried apple in a small pot and let simmer on your stove's lowest heat setting. (Do not leave stove unattended.) If using a potpourri pot, follow manufacturer's instructions. Replace water if contents seem dry.

HOLIDAY HOME SPRAY
(makes 4 2-ounce [60 ml] bottles)

1 cup (240 ml) distilled water

16 drops pine needle essential oil

8 drops cinnamon essential oil

4 drops mandarin essential oil

Nothing smells better around the holidays than the warm, spicy scent of pine, cinnamon, and citrus, and with this easy formula, you can make several little bottles to share with friends. Divide water among 4 2-ounce (60- ml) spray bottles. Add 4 drops pine needle essential oil, 2 drops cinnamon essential oil, and 1 drop mandarin essential oil to each bottle. Screw on the lids and shake well to distribute the oils.

Bathroom Brighteners

OF ALL THE ROOMS IN THE HOUSE WHERE DIRT AND ODOR ARE MOST DECIDEDLY UNWELCOME, bathrooms rank at the top of the list. But, unfortunately, bathrooms are by nature problematic because they tend to be smaller, sometimes poorly ventilated spaces where moisture lingers. This combination of wetness and warmth makes them perfect breeding grounds for bacteria and fungi; plus there are on occasion all kinds of other (ahem) unwelcome scents that require no further discussion.

However, if you've stocked up on some of the essential oils for the other formulas in this book, you can easily give your bathroom space an herbal makeover that will leave things more sanitary and decidedly more fragrant with just a few other household ingredients you probably already have on hand. You'll be following in a tradition that dates back to ancient times.

TEA-TREE OIL TUB AND TILE CLEANSER

1 cup (220 g) baking soda
¼ cup (60 ml) liquid castile soap
½ cup (120 ml) water
1 tablespoon (15 ml) vinegar
½ teaspoon (3 ml) tea-tree essential oil

Soap scum, hard water mineral deposits, and plain old dirt can eventually build up and leave their own unwanted story on your tub and tiles. Fortunately, there's a quick and easy formula you can put together to give your shower a proper scrub every week or two. Combine the baking soda and soap in a large bowl. Stir slowly until thoroughly mixed, then stir in the water (work slowly to avoid building a lot of lather). Add the vinegar and essential oil. Transfer the finished mixture to a squirt-top bottle. When using, shake mixture gently and apply with a damp sponge to clean surfaces. Rinse thoroughly with fresh water to avoid leaving a residue.

Tea tree

Tea-tree Oil

A BRIEF HISTORY

The tea tree is a fast-growing Australian evergreen native to New South Wales. The aboriginal peoples of Australia used its leaves to heal wounds and crushed them to make an inhalant. In 1772 Captain James Cook named it "Tea tree," after observing the native people make a tea from it. It is said that Cook's crew later drank their own version of the brew to combat scurvy. Not until studies done by Arthur Penfold in the 1920s revealed it to have powerful antimicrobial properties did tea-tree oil become widely used. With stronger antiseptic effects than carbolic acid (the common bactericide in use at the time), tea-tree oil became a staple of hospitals—during World War II, Australian soldiers carried it in their first-aid kits as a disinfectant.

Tea-tree oil is commonly added to soaps, creams, deodorants, and antifungal creams. When used topically, tea-tree oil can help prevent canker sores, as well as treat dandruff, acne, and foot fungus. It can be equally effective around the house to kill bacteria and fungi in hard-to-treat spaces such as bathrooms.

MAKING IT WORK FOR YOU

The tea tree is not widely grown outside its native swampy lowlands in Australia. Fortunately, tea-tree oil is widely available in health-food stores and online. Make sure to buy it from a reputable source and store it in a cool, dark place (like a medicine cabinet). Overexposure to light and heat will degrade it.

JUST-IN-THYME TUB SCRUB

¼ cup (55 g) baking soda
2 tablespoons (30 ml) liquid castile soap
10 drops thyme essential oil

Thyme is another valuable germ-fighting herb you'll want to include in your bathroom-cleaning arsenal. Here's a super-easy formula you can whip up in small batches and employ whenever you need to do a quick tub scrub. It is also effective on porcelain sinks and other nonporous surfaces. Combine the baking soda, soap, and essential oil in a small bowl. Stir to make a frosting-textured mixture. Use with a damp sponge to gently scrub away the grime, then rinse thoroughly with fresh water. If a smaller amount is desired, this formula can easily be cut in half.

Herb Fact

The thymus gland, a part of the lymphatic system, got its name from the herb thyme. It seems medieval doctors thought the gland resembled thyme leaves.

LEMON BALM SOFT SCRUB

1 cup (220 g) baking soda
1/3 cup (40 g) powdered milk
10 drops lemon balm essential oil
1/4 teaspoon (1.5 ml) liquid castile soap
Water, to make a paste

The powdered mix of this soft-scrub formula can be stored on your shelf indefinitely, so you can have a fresh supply handy whenever you need it. Combine the baking soda, powdered milk, and essential oil in a small plastic container with a tight-fitting lid. Shake vigorously to combine ingredients, and then set aside in a cool, dark place until you're ready to use. To make a batch of soft scrub, simply scoop a spoonful (or two) of the powdered mix into a small bowl. Add a squirt of liquid castile soap and just enough water to make a smooth paste. Use with a damp sponge to gently clean nonporous surfaces, and then rinse thoroughly with fresh water.

ON THE SPOT SALT SCRUBBER

2 teaspoons (10 ml) white vinegar

2 tablespoons (30 ml) salt

5 to 7 drops tea-tree essential oil

As evidenced by dozens of other formulas in this book, vinegar is a vital supply to have in the house; it's mildly acidic and a disinfectant, so it provides a safe, effective way to clean up a variety of messes and spills. But what about those times when vinegar needs a little boost? How can you amplify its scouring strength with other natural ingredients? Turn to the power of salt and tea-tree oil! Mix the vinegar and salt with the tea-tree oil to clean stubborn soap stains in your bathroom that need a stronger scrubbing. The tea-tree oil will leave its fresh scent. Double the batch if you need a larger supply, but don't worry about storing it—this formula costs practically nothing to produce. Rinse thoroughly after use.

EUCALYPTUS BATHROOM SANITIZER SPRAY

2 cups (475 ml) distilled water

1/4 cup (60 ml) vodka

1/2 teaspoon (3 ml) eucalyptus essential oil

The fresh, "green" scent and medicinal properties of eucalyptus make it a natural fit for the bathroom. To help keep your bathroom clean, try this homemade disinfectant spray. Combine the water, vodka, and essential oil in a plastic spray bottle and shake well. Lightly spray the surfaces you want to disinfect, then let air-dry. The eucalyptus oil will work its magic on your surfaces while imparting its welcome scent to your bathroom.

CITRUS WINDOW CLEANER

1 1/2 cups (350 ml) white vinegar

1/2 cup (120 ml) water

10 drops lemon or orange essential oil

Vinegar is a spectacular ingredient for many green home-cleaning formulas, but its sour scent can be off-putting. Though the vinegar scent will eventually fade as it dries, a little lemon or orange essential oil will help impart a familiar, fresh, and clean smell in its place. Combine the vinegar, water, and essential oil in a plastic spray bottle and shake well. Spray directly onto mirror or other glass surfaces, then wipe dry with a newspaper for a streak-free shine.

MOLD-FIGHTING SPRAY

¼ cup (60 ml) distilled water
1 teaspoon (5 ml) white vinegar
20 drops tea-tree essential oil

Mold and mildew pop up at inopportune times in inconvenient places, are hard to get rid of, and can leave behind tough stains. Essentially, they're an overgrowth of fungus spores. To keep your bathroom—or any other humidity-prone area of your house—clear of them, use this quick and easy spray on surfaces where they tend to grow. Combine the water, vinegar, and essential oil in a small plastic spray bottle and shake well. Spritz on walls, shower doors, and tubs, then let air-dry.

SHOWER CURTAIN LINER CLEANER

1 cup (220 g) baking soda
5 drops tea-tree oil

Beyond being unsightly, a dirty shower curtain liner is unhealthy. Every time you shower, you leave behind dead skin cells that become fodder for bacteria. Dampness also makes the liner an attractive place for household mold populations to multiply. Luckily, keeping that big sheet of plastic clean is pretty easy. Just toss the shower curtain liner into your washing machine, rings and all, along with 1 cup (220 g) baking soda and 5 drops tea-tree essential oil. No soap necessary. Let run through a gentle setting with warm water and hang in the shower to dry.

AIR FRESHENER

2 tablespoons (30 ml) isopropyl alcohol

1/4 cup (60 ml) water

1 tablespoon (15 ml) glycerin

10 drops grapefruit essential oil

10 drops lavender essential oil

5 drops peppermint essential oil

Many commercial bathroom fresheners have an overpowering scent. If you've amassed a collection of essential oils, you can create your own custom herbal formulas that can leave the air in your bathroom smelling sweet and fresh. Simply combine the isopropyl alcohol, water, glycerin and essential oils in a spray bottle (a decorative glass atomizer would be a great choice). Shake the bottle each time before using.

EVER-FRESH BATHROOM POTPOURRI

2 handfuls dried floral petals or citrus peels

1 cup (220 g) baking soda

10 to 15 drops essential oil of your choice

Use your favorite herbs to give your bathroom a signature scent. Try dried lavender petals and some drops of lavender essential oil. If you prefer citrus, choose lemon or orange peels. Combine petals or peels, baking soda, and essential oil in a decorative bowl. Stir gently every other day to release fragrance. Replenish monthly with more essential oil.

Wall, Carpet, Furniture, and Room Fresheners

IN OUR RUSHED AND BUSY MODERN LIFESTYLE, the old-fashioned notion of a thorough seasonal cleaning can fall by the wayside, but there are some important reasons why we should reconsider. Dust, mold, bacteria, and viruses, all of which are lurking in that sub-stuff dirt zone, can lead to some nasty health consequences if allowed to remain unchecked. And the fresh scents left behind by an herb-powered cleaning are both welcoming and mood-lifting.

Fortunately, many of the same cleaning formulas your grandparents might have learned (some of which have been handed down for centuries and longer) are still quite relevant today. That's because herbal home cleaning never goes out of style. What's more, using some herbs in your green cleaning solutions can actually help you feel reconnected to the rhythm of the natural world, especially if you take the time to grow and harvest your own antimicrobial and antifungal powerhouses...er, plants. As with all cleaning products, keep in mind it is always best to test on an inconspicuous area first.

ROSEMARY-LAVENDER RUG CLEANER

2 cups (440 g) baking soda

¼ cup (13 g) dried rosemary

¼ cup (12 g) dried lavender

10 to 20 drops lavender essential oil, optional

Long before wall-to-wall carpet was even an idea in some interior decorator's mind, people used herbs to refresh their flooring. In colonial America, a popular cleaning strategy (adapted from the European tradition of strewing herbs) was to scatter fresh herbs in a room and then stomp on them as a way to release the plants' essential oils before sweeping them up. Fortunately, you don't have to go to such extremes these days. Simply mix up a batch of this odor-fighting baking soda blend that's a great alternative to store-bought carpet fresheners. Combine the baking soda, rosemary, dried lavender, and essential oil, if using, in a jar with a tight-fitting lid. Let sit for several weeks so that the scents can combine. To use, scatter ¼ cup (55 g) at a time on carpet and let sit for 10 to 15 minutes to absorb odors. Vacuum as usual.

Rosemary

A BRIEF HISTORY

Native to the Mediterranean region, rosemary has long been a popular herb not only in the kitchen but outside it. The ancient Greeks believed that rosemary improved the memory; students wore garlands of rosemary to help them remember better. The herb was also used ceremonially, at funerals to help survivors remember the departed and in weddings to symbolize the life the bride led before her union. In Hamlet, Shakespeare had Ophelia note, "There's rosemary, that's for remembrance."

Rosemary's strong aroma made it a popular spice in Mediterranean cuisines. It was also used to preserve meat. Today, rosemary is found in a variety of herbal beauty aids, from shampoo to facial scrubs. Its piney scent also makes rosemary essential oil a perfect fit for a variety of home-improvement products.

MAKING IT WORK FOR YOU

Fresh rosemary is generally available year-round in most grocery stores. However, you might enjoy growing it. (If you live in a cooler climate, it will be an annual.) Purchase garden transplants or propagate from stem tip cuttings. Plant your rosemary in a sunny, well-drained site. Rosemary also grows well in a container. Keep plants evenly moist. Do not allow them to dry out. In autumn, plant in fresh potting mix and bring indoors to enjoy throughout the winter.

VACUUM REFRESHER

5 to 10 drops lemon essential oil

5 to 10 drops eucalyptus essential oil

If you have indoor pets, you've probably had the experience of vacuuming your carpet only to have an overwhelming pet smell fill the room afterward. This occurs because the odor from pet hair can intensify in the closed, confined space of a partially used vacuum cleaner bag. The odor is then released when the vacuum is used. Fortunately, there's a remarkably easy solution that won't require you to replace the expensive bags every time you pull out your machine. Sprinkle the essential oils on half a tissue or a few pieces of toilet paper. Place the tissue in the vacuum bag (or let the machine do the work and suck it up). Repeat every week or two, if needed, to replace that pet odor with a fresh, clean scent.

CARPET SPOT CLEANER

½ cup dried thyme

1 cup (240 ml) white vinegar

2 cups (475 ml) water

1 tablespoon (15 ml) liquid castile soap

Here's a gentle and effective way to spot-clean your carpet in between shampoos. Begin by combining the thyme and vinegar in a wide-mouth glass bottle with a tight-fitting lid. Store in a cool, dark place for approximately 2 weeks. Shake the jar gently every day or two. After the 2 weeks have passed, strain the mixture through a small sieve lined with a coffee filter or cheesecloth. Transfer vinegar to a plastic storage bottle and add the water and castile soap. Use a soft brush and a towel with a few tablespoons of this mixture to gently brush at non-oily stains that have collected on your carpet and ease the stain away (test on an inconspicuous area first). Blot dry.

ALL-NATURAL WALL WASH

4 cups (950 ml) warm water
¼ cup (60 ml) white vinegar
¼ teaspoon (1 ml) lavender essential oil

Back in the day, fireplaces, coal heat, cigarette smoke, and cooking grease left a tangible film upon walls that made wall cleaning an annual chore for most households. These days, we don't have to spend as much time scrubbing down all the walls, but dirt and grime still have a tendency to collect in key spots. To keep surface dirt under control, keep a bottle of this formula handy. The lavender essential oil will help cut the smell of the vinegar. Combine the water, vinegar, and essential oil in a plastic bottle with a spray pump lid. Shake vigorously before using, then spray directly onto surface area to be cleaned. Wipe gently with a damp sponge.

CEILING FAN CLEANER

½ cup (24 g) dried lavender
1 cup (240 ml) white vinegar
½ cup (120 ml) water

Ceiling fans provide such an important function in a house, circulating a gentle breeze and stabilizing the temperature of a room. It can be easy to overlook the amount of dust and grease that can collect on the fan blades when they're in use. For an effective dust and grease-fighting cleanser, combine the lavender and vinegar in a wide-mouth glass bottle with a tight-fitting lid (a large jelly jar works well). Store in a cool, dark place for approximately 2 weeks. Shake the jar gently every day or two so that contents don't settle. After the 2 weeks have passed, strain the mixture through a small sieve lined with a coffee filter or cheesecloth. Transfer vinegar to a plastic storage bottle and add the water. To use, turn off fans; dampen a soft, lint-free towel with a few tablespoons of vinegar mixture; and wipe fan blades clean. Let air-dry. Vinegar also discourages static electricity, so the blades will stay cleaner longer.

SWEET DREAMS BED-BUG SPRAY

½ cup (120 ml) distilled water
2 tablespoons (30 ml) vodka
10 drops lavender essential oil

When you're traveling, the last thing you want to think about at night is what else might be sharing the bed with you. If you're looking for a natural way to keep the bed bugs at bay, pack up a little spray bottle of lavender water. Combine the water, vodka, and essential oil in a small plastic bottle with a spray pump lid. Shake vigorously before using, then spray lightly but liberally onto bedding and pillows, as well as carpets and any drapes that surround the bed.

LEMON-MINT MATTRESS REFRESHER

½ cup (17 g) dried mint
½ cup (17 g) dried lemon balm
1 cup (220 g) baking soda

Whether you're trying to instill a little life into your old mattress or are looking for a way to insure a borrowed bed feels like home, here's an easy herbal solution to try. Use a blender or food processor to grind the mint and lemon balm into fine pieces. Mix with baking soda and store for 1 or 2 weeks to allow scents to combine. To use, scatter half of the mixture lightly over the top of your bare mattress. If you use a mattress cover, put herbs directly on top of that. Cover with a clean, fitted sheet.

Mint

Mint originated in the Mediterranean. For the ancient Romans, it was a symbol of hospitality: they strewed it around their banquet tables during feasts as a welcoming gesture to their guests. As written by the 16th-century herbalist John Gerarde, Pliny the Elder is reported to have noted, "The smell of mint does stir up the mind and the taste to a greedy desire of meate." Mint quickly spread throughout the world, and has long been used both medicinally and in the cuisines of numerous cultures. So well known was mint that it was even mentioned in literature, with references in Chaucer and Shakespeare. The 17th-century herbalist Culpeper noted mint as a useful remedy for more than thirty different conditions. In North America, the Shoshone Indians learned to make good use of mint by brewing tea from the dried leaves and stems; they found it was especially useful for relieving gas pains.

More recently, studies have shown that mint can calm stomach and intestinal upsets. It also possesses antimicrobial properties.

Commercially, peppermint is one of the most common flavorings that we associate with clean, fresh breath, and it is used in everything from chewing gum to toothpaste. Herbalists have long suggested mint for stomach problems because it may have a relaxing effect on the muscles in the digestive tract. A cup of mint tea can help ease flatulence, improve digestion, and quell feelings of nausea.

Mint is an especially easy-to-grow perennial that does well in full sun to partial shade, so it is a good starter plant for the beginning herb gardener. That said, there are quite a number of different kinds to consider. Among the most commonly used in cooking and healing are peppermint and spearmint. Peppermint has dark green leaves with a reddish stem and lavender flowers; spearmint has lighter green, pointy leaves and pink flowers and is usually the milder-tasting of the two. Both types can grow up to two feet (61 cm) tall and become quite invasive. So unless you have a lot of extra garden space to spare, you might want to keep your mint plants confined to containers.

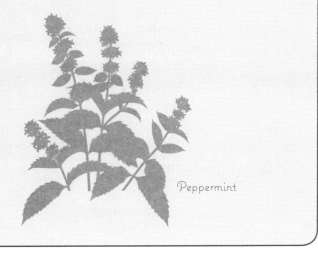

Peppermint

LAVENDER FURNITURE WAX

¼ cup (60 g) beeswax
1 teaspoon (5 ml) lavender essential oil

You can usually buy beeswax where woodworking supplies are sold because it is a common ingredient in homemade wax polishes and an excellent, light lubricant for wooden moving parts. Although the scent of beeswax is pleasant by itself, adding a whiff of lavender to the mix will give you a distinct custom combination that might even make housework more relaxing. Melt the beeswax in a small saucepan over low heat. Stir in lavender oil. Pour mixture into a shallow glass container, then allow to harden. Use as you would a commercial furniture wax, applying a thin coat with a soft cotton cloth and buffing to a warm glow.

LEMON-FRESH WOODWORK CLEANER

2 tablespoons (30 ml) fresh lemon juice
¼ cup (60 ml) olive oil

For furniture and woodwork with an old-fashioned finish (i.e., an oiled instead of shiny varnish), make your own furniture polish to ensure a bright shine. Combine the lemon juice and olive oil in a glass jar with a tight-fitting lid. Shake vigorously to combine ingredients, and then apply to furniture with a soft cotton cloth.

DUST-FIGHTING ROOM SPRAY

¼ cup (60 ml) water

¼ cup (60 ml) vodka

20 drops essential oil of your choice

One of the ironies of housecleaning is the amount of debris that can linger in the air long after a good round of vacuuming and sweeping. For people with indoor allergies, this can be decidedly unpleasant. To minimize the dust haze and help things settle down faster after cleaning, consider making a batch of this fresh-scented room spray. You can even customize the formula if you like with your favorite mix of essential oils—you might try a warm combination of cinnamon, clove, and orange for autumn, or a floral bouquet of lavender and rose for spring and summer. Whatever mix of essential oils you choose, fill a 4-ounce (120 ml) spray bottle with equal parts vodka and water, and then add about 20 drops essential oil. Shake well before using and spray generously as the finishing step of your housecleaning routine, filling the air with a light mist that will trap floating air particles as it settles.

PURIFYING SAGE FIRE-STARTER

Fresh sage
Cotton twine or string
Old newspaper

In many Native American traditions, sage is considered a sacred herb and burning it is believed to release a purifying energy that can cleanse a space of negative spirits or feelings. Most people would be hard-pressed not to find sage's woodsy scent appealing. Cut long stems of fresh sage. Gather into bunches and secure in bundles by tying their stems together with cotton twine. Hang upside down in a hot, dry space (your garage or attic rafters are ideal). When they are dry, wrap the bundles loosely in sheets of old newspaper and stack neatly until ready to use. Tuck a few beneath your logs when you're ready to start a fire, then light the newspaper ends as kindling.

Sage

Sage

Native to the Mediterranean area, sage is featured in the writings of Theophrastus and Pliny the Elder, who recommended it for its diuretic effects. Early Greek physicians reported that sage could be used to stop bleeding and clean ulcers and sores, as well as treat hoarseness and coughs. Sage has a long and continuous history of medicinal use, right up through the present age. In fact, sage was officially listed in the United States Pharmacopoeia from 1840 to 1900 and has been used effectively for treating throat infections, dental abscesses, infected gums, and mouth ulcers. This powerful herb can fight a variety of infections, killing bacteria as well as viruses, and fighting inflammation along the way. New research indicates that sage may also play a role in improving memory.

Sage is a reliable remedy for sore throats and canker sores. The volatile oils in sage are thought to be largely responsible for most of this herb's beneficial properties, so keep your cup covered when brewing tea (fewer volatile oils will evaporate that way).

MAKING IT WORK FOR YOU

Sage is a hardy herb that usually thrives better outside. It grows well almost anywhere, but it definitely prefers good drainage and full sun. If you want to dry your sage, harvest the leaves before the flower buds open. Once dry, store in an airtight container, allowing the herb to last until your next growing season.

Herbs Outside the Home

THE USEFULNESS OF HERBS is by no means limited to what we can do with them once we take them indoors. In fact, there are many wonderful ways herbs make our lives a little easier outside the home, too.

In ancient times, both the Egyptians and Romans burned herbs to keep pests at bay. Strongly scented herbs were used to discourage infestations of mice and other vermin. Today, herbal pest repellents offer natural alternatives to commercial products, which are often high in toxins.

In addition to their practical uses, herbs were also used decoratively and symbolically—herbal wreaths, worn by the ancient Romans, evolved into symbols of welcome to be placed on doors and windows.

Through the centuries, aromatic herbs were also used to line pathways; when walked upon, they released a pleasant scent—which led to the practice of strewing herbs in enclosed spaces to freshen the air. These traditions continue today, and there are plenty of modern adaptations you can try.

In this section, you will find ideas for ways to use herbal solutions outside the home, whether you need to repel insects, reduce odors in the car, or clean and restore your hands after an afternoon of hard work in the garden.

And finally, notwithstanding the myriad uses of herbs, it won't surprise you to know that many people consider the art of herb gardening to be a worthwhile pursuit unto itself!

GARLIC-PEPPER BUG SPRAY

1 large onion, coarsely chopped

1 head garlic cloves, peeled and roughly chopped

2 tablespoons (30 ml) dried red pepper flakes

1 cup (240 ml) water

1 teaspoon (5 ml) liquid castile soap

If you're looking for a more natural method of pest control in your garden, make this formula part of your arsenal. The combination of volatile oils from the pepper and garlic will render most of your plants inhospitable to cabbage worms, caterpillars, hornworms, aphids, flea beetles, and other insects. Wash your hands thoroughly after use since this is not a formula you want to get anywhere near your face, eyes, or other delicate areas of your body. Place the onion, garlic, and red pepper flakes in a blender or food processor. Combine, then slowly add the water until contents are liquefied. Transfer mixture to a gallon-size (4-l) container (e.g., a clean, empty milk jug) and fill with soap. Refrigerate for several days. To use, pour a cup (240 ml) of the liquid through a strainer and into a 32-ounce (950-ml) spray bottle. Fill with water and liberally spray the plants you want to protect. Repeat regularly, especially after it rains. Keep refrigerated.

Herb Fact
During World War I, battlefield doctors often used raw garlic to treat soldiers' infected wounds.

LEMON BALM-EUCALYPTUS BUG REPELLENT

2 tablespoons (30 ml) light olive oil

1 tablespoon (15 ml) aloe vera gel, optional

15 drops lemon balm essential oil

10 drops eucalyptus essential oil

This antibug formula is well suited for skin. The lemon balm will help keep mosquitoes at bay; the aroma from the splash of eucalyptus can help ward off black flies and ticks. Combine the olive oil, aloe vera gel, if used, and essential oils in a small jar with a tight-fitting lid. Shake vigorously until ingredients are well combined, then apply generously to exposed skin before going outside.

LEMON-FRESH CAR CLEANING SPRAY

1-$\frac{1}{2}$ cups (350 ml) white vinegar

$\frac{1}{2}$ cup (120 ml) water

10 drops lemon essential oil

Use this simple formula to give your car's windshield, chrome, and mirrors a streak-free shine. Combine the vinegar, water, and essential oil in a plastic spray bottle, then shake well. Spray directly onto mirror or other glass surfaces and wipe dry with a newspaper. Use a soft cloth when cleaning chrome.

ODOR- AND STRESS-RELIEVING LAVENDER CAR SACHET

1 cup (48 g) dried lavender
20 drops lavender essential oil
1 clean handkerchief, preferably cotton or linen
1 rubber band

A musty-smelling car is never pleasant. Add the hassle of traffic and you may feel your anxiety levels regularly peaking as you sit in your car waiting to move. Consider turning to the power of herbal aromatherapy to freshen the air and restore your sense of calm. Lavender is notable for its stress-relieving effects, and this discreet sachet can be stored in your glove compartment or hung from the rearview mirror. Combine the lavender and essential oil in a large bowl and toss to coat. Place ingredients in the center of the handkerchief and gather the corners together. Secure the center with a rubber band, making sure the contents are a little loose to promote better airflow.

Lavender

GARDENER'S HAND CREAM

2 tablespoons (30 ml) beeswax
1 tablespoon (15 ml) coconut oil
¼ cup (60 ml) vitamin E oil
1 tablespoon (15 ml) calendula tincture
5 drops lavender essential oil
¼ teaspoon (1 ml) baking soda

Even if you wear gloves, a day spent working in the garden can take a toll on your hands, leaving them dried, scratched, and sore. The beeswax and coconut oil in this hand cream make a remarkably soothing combination, and the addition of calendula and lavender will help treat minor skin irritations swiftly. Place the beeswax and coconut oil in a small glass bowl and warm slowly in the microwave, heating for 10 seconds at a time, just until melted. Stir in the vitamin E oil, calendula tincture, lavender essential oil, and baking soda. Mix until smooth and allow to cool slightly before pouring into a sterile jar.

Herb Fact

Coconut oil is extracted from the mature coconuts of the coconut palm tree.

GARDENER'S HAND SOAP

1 bar glycerin soap, coarsely grated

2 tablespoons (30 ml) coarse yellow cornmeal

½ teaspoon (3 ml) lavender essential oil

Here's a great way to refashion a plain bar of glycerin soap into something strong enough to help clean your hands after a long day in the garden. The cornmeal boosts the scrubbing potential, and the lavender essential oil imparts a gentle fragrance. Heat the grated soap gently over a double boiler until melted. Add the cornmeal and essential oil and stir briskly. Transfer mixture to a soap mold of your choice. Allow it to cool and set according to the soap mold manufacturer's instructions.

EUCALYPTUS BUG-BANISHING GARDEN SPRAY

2 cups (475 ml) water

2 teaspoons (10 ml) canola oil

½ teaspoon (3 ml) eucalyptus essential oil

¼ teaspoon (1 ml) liquid castile soap

If your garden is prone to aphids, earwigs, slugs, or beetles, this spray is easy to put together and can be used safely on plants that pests seem to love most, including roses, tomatoes, cucumbers, and strawberries. Combine the water, canola oil, eucalyptus oil, and soap in a large spray bottle and shake vigorously. Spray plants thoroughly at the first sign of pests and repeat every 3 to 5 days until problem subsides. For best results, make a fresh batch every time.

Herb Fact
Canola oil comes from the rapeseed plant.

MARIGOLD BUG SPRAY

½ cup (120 ml) marigold flowers
¼ cup (60 ml) fresh cilantro
1 quart (1 liter) water
1 teaspoon (5 ml) dishwashing liquid

Many garden designers love to include hardy marigold borders in their plans because these colorful flowers can help protect nearby plants from a variety of bugs and pests, including beetles, tomato hornworms, whiteflies, and mosquitoes. However, if you want to extend the bug-repelling properties of marigold to other parts of your outdoor living space, try this simple formula. Combine the marigold, cilantro, and 1 cup of the water in a food processor and whirl. Transfer to a covered container, add another cup water to the mix and refrigerate for 24 hours. Line a colander with a paper towel or coffee filter and strain mixture into a spray bottle. Add remaining 2 cups water and dishwashing liquid. Shake vigorously to combine and spray generously on other plants and patio spaces (the mixture may stain light-colored fabrics, so test in an inconspicuous area first). This spray will keep for about a week if refrigerated between uses.

Cilantro

ANTS ANTIDOTE

2 cups (475 ml) water

2 cups (475 ml) fresh mint or 20 drops peppermint essential oil

In the great outdoors, ants are vital to a healthy lawn. They help "clean the scene below the green," but when they start to venture indoors, it can be another story altogether. If ants have found their way into your indoor living spaces, use the power of mint to interrupt the trails they leave for one another. Simply bring the water to a gentle boil and steep the mint in the water for 10 to 15 minutes. Let cool to room temperature, then strain into a spray bottle. Spray generously around entryways and any other places where you've spotted your unwelcome visitors. If fresh mint is not available, you can mix 20 drops of peppermint essential oil in the same amount of water.

Peppermint

PATIO FURNITURE CLEANER

10 drops eucalyptus essential oil

¼ cup (55 g) baking soda

1 quart (1 liter) water

Getting your patio ready for summer usually entails a bit of furniture scrubbing, so why not bring some herb power to the equation? Simply add eucalyptus oil to the baking soda and stir to combine. Add to a quart of warm water and use this herb-scented mix to wash down all of your outdoor chairs and tables. Rinse thoroughly with fresh water when you're done.

Herb Fact

Baking soda originally was derived from a mineral called nahcolite. Much of it is now made synthetically.

Pet Care

AS ANY PET OWNER KNOWS, sometimes our four-legged friends seem very wise in navigating the natural world. Have you ever watched your dog or cat eat grass? According to some pet experts, grass may be an animal's instinctive remedy for a gassy or upset stomach. Similarly, animals may be drawn to eat herbs in the wild that can assist their digestion. Less practically, cat owners are likely well aware of the effect of catmint (also known as catnip) on felines, but did you know that dogs react strongly to the smell of anise?

It makes sense, then, that there are many herb-related pet care strategies. For example, the ancient Greeks used herbs such as pennyroyal and rosemary to repel fleas, while the Maori used tea-tree oil—and you can, too. If you are trying to reduce your household exposure to chemicals, you'll want to try some of the natural, herbal pet care formulas that you will find in this section. Keep in mind, however, that some plants that are perfectly safe for people may be poisonous for pets, so be vigilant about protecting your beloved pet. Don't assume that all remedies in this book (aside from those mentioned in this Pet Care section) are safe to administer to your pet without first consulting a vet.

CAT DETERRENT FORMULA

Peel of 1 orange
1 cup (220 g) baking soda
1 cup (48 g) dried lavender

Using herbal products with cats is tricky because their livers are incapable of metabolizing the volatile oils, so avoid using all essential oil products around your cat. You can, however, safely use the power of herbs to help control certain problem behavior. Cats detest the smell of oranges and lavender, so consider this formula if your cat repeatedly soils your favorite rug or carpet. Remove the skin from the orange and combine the peels, baking soda and lavender; store the mixture for about a week in a container with a tight-fitting lid. After you've cleaned and treated the soiled area, spread the mixture evenly over any spots where your cat has left his mark. Let mixture sit for 24 hours, then vacuum thoroughly. Your cat should be disinclined to make the same mistake twice.

Herb Fact

Catnip, also known as catmint, belongs to the genus *Nepeta*, which has more than 200 species.

CRAZY CAT CATNIP TOY

Denim fabric

1 bunch dried catnip

Many cats respond well to catnip; think of it like an after-work cocktail for cats, temporarily relieving them of stress and nervousness. Cut 2 3-inch (8-cm) squares out of an old pair of jeans. Place one square on top of the other, then sew 3 of the sides together, leaving a $3/8$-inch (1-cm) seam around the outside edge. Turn inside out and fill with dried catnip. Sew the open side closed and watch your cat have a blast playing with her new toy.

NATURAL FLEA COLLAR

Bandanna

10 to 15 drops tea-tree essential oil

10 to 15 drops eucalyptus essential oil

Sure, Fido looks cute wearing a colorful bandanna, but did you know that scarf can do double duty as a natural flea collar? The combination of tea-tree and eucalyptus essential oils can help keep a variety of pests, especially fleas, from bothering your dog. Generously sprinkle a bandanna with the essential oils, let dry, and then fasten around your pet's neck as usual. For maximum protection, refresh weekly. This remedy is only appropriate for dogs. Do not use essential oils on cats. Do consult with your vet to make sure it is appropriate for your situation.

FLEA-REMOVING CARPET CURE

2 cups (440 g) baking soda
1 cup (43 g) dried pennyroyal, crushed

The egg of a flea can hatch in two weeks or lay dormant for up to eight months, and given that female fleas lay about twenty eggs per day, and up to six hundred in a lifetime, it is easy to see why getting rid of them can be so challenging. If you want to rid your home of fleas the natural route, persistence is crucial. Fortunately, herbs like pennyroyal, a long-standing resource for pest control, can help. Combine the baking soda and pennyroyal in a jar with a tight-fitting lid, then shake to incorporate ingredients. At night, remove pets from the room and vacuum affected area; sprinkle carpet lightly with baking soda mixture and let sit overnight. In the morning, vacuum thoroughly again and dispose of the vacuum bag. Do check with your vet to make sure pennyroyal is appropriate for your situation.

DOG BED ODOR ELIMINATOR

2 cups (440 g) baking soda
1 teaspoon (5 ml) eucalyptus essential oil

If your dog's bed seems in need of a little scent refreshment, this easy odor eliminator might do the trick. Combine the baking soda and eucalyptus oil in a jar with a tight-fitting lid, and shake to incorporate ingredients. Scatter a few spoonfuls on your dog's bed to keep odors at bay in between washings. This remedy is only appropriate for dogs. Do not use essential oils on cats.

GENTLE ALOE DOG SHAMPOO

1/2 cup (120 ml) liquid castile soap
1/4 cup (60 ml) aloe vera gel
1/2 cup (120 ml) water
1/4 teaspoon (1 ml) rosemary essential oil, optional

The ingredients in this natural shampoo are well suited to your dog's needs: the rosemary essential oil works as a natural flea repellent and the aloe vera gel helps prevent painful fur tangles. In a large bowl, stir together the soap and aloe vera gel gently (you won't make too many suds). Stir in the water and essential oil, if using. Transfer the mixture to an empty shampoo bottle and label it clearly with your pet's name. Shampoo and rinse your dog as usual. This remedy is only appropriate for dogs. Do not use essential oils on cats.

FUR-BRIGHTENING PET RINSE

2 cups (475 ml) water

1 teaspoon (5 ml) dried or 1 tablespoon (15 ml) fresh rosemary

1/2 cup (120 ml) white vinegar

Rosemary tea is an excellent conditioner that promotes a shiny coat and helps repel fleas. This recipe is suitable for dogs and cats. Bring the water to a gentle boil, add the rosemary, and simmer for about 10 minutes. Remove from heat and let steep for 30 more minutes, or until room temperature. Strain, then stir in the vinegar. To use, pour the rinse over your pet's freshly washed and rinsed fur. Massage into the fur gently and towel dry. Do not rinse.

ITCH-RELIEVING HERBAL DIP FOR DOGS

1/2 gallon (2 l) water

2 cups (48 g) fresh peppermint, packed

This herbal dip is especially soothing in the summer if your dog is show-ing signs of itchiness and fleas. Bring half of the water to a gentle boil, add the peppermint, then remove from heat. Let steep for 30 more minutes, or until room temperature. Strain and stir in the remaining water. To use, pour the rinse over your dog's freshly brushed fur (this dip does not require giving the dog a bath first). Massage gently and towel dry. Do not rinse. Repeat every 3 to 4 days as necessary. This remedy is only appropriate for dogs. Do not use essential oils on cats.

MIGHTY EAR MITE FIGHTER

1 cup (48 g) dried chamomile
1 cup (240 ml) white vinegar
Distilled water

Ear mites are a common and irritating problem for many pets. Essentially, they are tiny, infectious parasites that set up shop in your cat or dog's ear canals and feast on earwax and skin oil. Over time, they can lead to infection and are best diagnosed and treated properly by your pet's vet. To keep your pet's ear canals clean, however, try this ear wash that will help soothe itching and inflammation, and make those pesky mites find your pet's ears far less hospitable. Place chamomile in a clean glass jar with a tight-fitting, nonmetallic lid, then cover with vinegar. Store in a cool, dark place for 2 weeks, shaking the jar every day or two so contents remain active. Strain the liquid into a different clean jar and mix with an equal amount of distilled water. Soak a cotton ball or clean rag in this solution, then use it to gently wipe in and around your pet's ears.

Safe-Use Guide for Herbs and Essential Oils in This Book

While the formulas in this book have been drawn from reliable sources and are generally safe for most adults, you should be aware of the following cautions that apply to some herbs and essential oils. As with any over-the-counter remedies, talk with your doctor before using herbs if you are under a physician's care for any condition, taking other medications, pregnant, or nursing. Check with your pediatrician before giving herbal remedies to children. Discontinue use if you experience any unusual reactions.

ALOE VERA: Not for use on surgical incisions as it may delay wound healing. Do not take internally.

BURDOCK: Do not use if you are pregnant. May trigger allergies in those sensitive to daisies, ragweed, or chrysanthemums.

CALENDULA: Avoid if you are pregnant or nursing.

CAYENNE: Do not use on an empty stomach, as it may irritate the gastrointestinal tract. Do not use near eyes.

CHAMOMILE: May trigger an allergic reaction in people allergic to ragweed, asters, and chrysanthemums.

CINNAMON: Use caution if you take blood-thinning or glucose-lowering medication.

CLOVE (ESSENTIAL OIL): Do not use for more than 2 weeks at a time.

COMFREY: Do not take internally. Not for use on deep or infected wounds because it can promote surface healing before underlying tissue has been sufficiently repaired.

ECHINACEA: May trigger an allergic reaction in people allergic to ragweed, asters, and chrysanthemums. Use caution if you have an autoimmune condition.

EUCALYPTUS (ESSENTIAL OIL): Do not use for more than 2 weeks at a time. May irritate the skin if not properly diluted. Do not use if you are pregnant or nursing. Check with your doctor if you have asthma.

GARLIC: Discontinue use 7 days before surgery.

GOLDENSEAL: Do not use if you have high blood pressure or if you are pregnant or nursing.

GINGER: Dried root or powder may increase bile secretions in people with gallstones when used in therapeutic amounts. Safe when used in cooking.

LICORICE ROOT: Do not use if you have low potassium levels, diabetes, hypertension, or liver or kidney disorders. Do not use daily for more than 4 to 6 weeks because overuse can lead to water retention, hypertension related to low potassium, or impaired heart and kidney function.

PENNYROYAL: Do not ingest; do not use if you are pregnant or nursing.

RHUBARB: Do not use if you have kidney dysfunction. Only the stalk is edible; the leaves are toxic.

ROSEMARY (ESSENTIAL OIL): Do not use if you have hypertension, ulcerative colitis, or epilepsy. Do not ingest.

SAGE: Do not use if you have hypoglycemia or are undergoing anticonvulsant therapy. May increase the sedative side effects of some drugs when used in therapeutic amounts. Safe when used in cooking.

SLIPPERY ELM: May interfere with absorption of some medications, so take separately.

TEA (GREEN): Limit consumption to 2 cups (475 ml) of green tea per day if you have been diagnosed with an irregular heartbeat; caffeine and other alkaloids can speed up heart rates. Also, limit consumption if you have stomach ulcers; its bitter taste stimulates gastric acid production.

TEA-TREE OIL: Do not ingest.

WHITE WILLOW BARK: Follow the same cautions as you would for aspirin.

YLANG-YLANG (ESSENTIAL OIL): Use in moderation; its strong smell can cause nausea or headaches when used in copious amounts.

Index

Recipe titles are capitalized

About the Author

SHEA ZUKOWSKI is an editor and writer specializing in earth-friendly information and natural living. A former senior editor for Rodale Books, she spent years seeking out the best advice related to cooking, health, nutrition, and pets. She lives in the blissfully quiet town of Emmaus, Pennsylvania, with her husband and two sons.